Cultivating Your Landscape!!

"A path to purpose, Clarity and JOY"

By Lea Monera

" Dedicated to my beloved God for all of its daily blessings!! To my family, and good friends!! To you my dear reader!! And all those people who supported me unconditionally throughout my walking paths in my life and my careers. Even though some of them didn't even realize they were doing it."

Prologue

This book is a practical and emotionally supportive guide for those seeking to cultivate their peace of mind, well-being, and personal growth. Through a variety of techniques and strategies, readers will learn to better explore and understand their own cognitive landscape, overcome obstacles, and achieve greater clarity, purpose, and happiness in their lives.

The ideal reader of this book could be people of any age, independent minded, people interested in taking care of all aspects of their body, mind and soul. And learn to take care of the people around them , as well as themselves. It can be for people from any working background, or those who work in the health sector, for a man with concerns and attitudes towards aspects of developing emotional intelligence, and get to know a bit more the functionality of the human mind, a progressive woman with concerns on developing her cognitive aspects of the mind, or a transgender with an awaken, open mind and willing to learn, growth and evolve mentally and spirituality. Mental renewal is necessary just as we will update a computer, just as if it were a high precision machine, otherwise our mind could become obsolete.

CONTENTS

Chapter 1

Unveiling Your Cognitive Landscape Exploring the Interconnectedness of Mind, Body and Spirit

As an International Qualified Health Care Assistant, passionate about my work and dedicated to supporting the health and wellness of others, I understand the profound significance of self-awareness in my personal and professional journey. This journey invites you to embark on a transformative exploration of the intricate tapestry that weaves together your mind, body, and spirit, empowering you to cultivate a deeper understanding of yourself and the world around you.

In a formal, yet friendly and engaging tone, we will delve into the fundamental principles of self-awareness, guiding you through a comprehensive examination of the interconnectedness that lies at the heart of your cognitive landscape.

By delving into the intricate interplay between your mental, physical, and spiritual dimensions, you will uncover the profound insights that can unlock your full potential and propel you towards the realization of your career goals whichever they are. Mine are mainly to become a registered nurse (one of these days), among other goals. Through a series of thought-provoking exercises and insightful reflections, you will embark on a journey of self-discovery, shedding light on the complex web of emotions, beliefs, and experiences that shape your unique perspective. This process will not only deepen your understanding of yourself but also equip you with the tools to navigate the challenges and opportunities that arise in your personal and professional life.

As a healthcare professional, I understand the importance of holistic well-being, and this chapter will demonstrate how cultivating self-awareness can enhance your ability to provide compassionate and effective care to those that you care for, and for your patients. By aligning your mind, body, and spirit, you will develop a heightened sensitivity to the needs of those you attend and serve, empowering you to deliver the highest quality of care and contribute to the overall well-being of your patients, family, friends, colleagues, and community.

Whether you are drawn to the metaphysical, the comedic, or the suspenseful, this journey will captivate your imagination and inspire you to embrace the power of self-awareness.

Through engaging narratives, thought-provoking insights, and practical strategies, you will uncover the transformative potential that lies within, paving the way for a more fulfilling and purposeful life. As you embark with me on this journey of self-discovery, it would be good to point out that my experiences and perspectives, have been shaped by my travels across five continents, will serve as a rich tapestry of inspiration, guiding you towards a deeper understanding of yourself and the world around you. Embrace the power of self-awareness, and unlock the boundless possibilities that await you on the path towards your aspirations , as I am challenging myself to become a registered nurse, among other things I want to achieve.

I will begin to explain the fundamental principles of self-awareness and how cultivating it can deepen one's understanding of the intricate relationship between the mind, body, and spirit. Discuss how aligning the mind, body, and spirit can enhance one's overall well-being and ability to provide compassionate, effective care as a healthcare professional.

Emphasize the importance of holistic well-being and how addressing all three aspects - mental, physical, and spiritual - can unlock one's full potential and support the realization of career goals. Provide practical strategies and exercises that encourage the reader to explore the interconnectedness of their cognitive landscape, such as mindfulness practices, reflective journaling, and body-mind-spirit integration techniques. Highlight how the reader's diverse life experiences, including their travels across five continents, can serve as a rich source of inspiration and insight as they embark on this journey of self-discovery.

Emphasize the transformative power of self-awareness and how it can lead to a more fulfilling and purposeful life, both personally and professionally.

The Mind-Body Connection

At the heart of self-awareness lies the profound understanding of the intricate connection between your mind and body.

As you delve deeper into this relationship, you will uncover the powerful ways in which your thoughts, emotions, and beliefs directly impact your physical well-being.

Through the practice of mindfulness, you will learn to observe the subtle interplay between your mental state and bodily sensations.

By tuning into the present moment and cultivating a non-judgmental awareness of your inner experience, you will develop the ability to recognize patterns and triggers that influence your overall health and vitality.

Engaging in regular mindfulness exercises, such as breath awareness and body scans, will help you to identify areas of tension or imbalance within your physical form. As you bring your attention to these areas with compassion and curiosity, you will create the space for healing and restoration to occur naturally.

Moreover, by acknowledging the profound impact of your thoughts and emotions on your physical well-being, you will be empowered to make conscious choices that support your health. Through the practice of positive affirmations, visualization, and cognitive reframing, you can reshape limiting beliefs and cultivate a mindset that fosters resilience, adaptability, and overall well-being.

Here are some common misconceptions about the mind-body-spirit connection that I should have address in Chapter 1:

1. **The mind, body, and spirit:** Are separate entities that function independently. In reality, they are deeply interconnected and influence each other profoundly.

2. **The mind has magical or all-powerful control:** Over the body and the external world. While thoughts and emotions can significantly impact physical health, there is no scientific evidence to support the idea that the mind can shape reality through "intentions" or "positive thinking" alone.

3. **The mind-body connection:** Is a new age or pseudoscientific concept. In fact, neuroscience has firmly established that brain activity interacts with the body through the nervous system, endocrine system, and immune system, with significant effects on health and well-being.

4. **Addressing the nervous system:** With medication or medical procedures is sufficient to restore health.

Many illnesses have their roots in unresolved emotional and spiritual issues that also need to be addressed.

5. **The body is a machine that functions independently of the mind and spirit**: In reality, the body is a sacred temple that houses our eternal being and should be treated with reverence and care.

By addressing these misconceptions and emphasizing the scientific evidence supporting the mind-body-spirit connection, you can help readers develop a more holistic understanding of health and well-being. This foundation will set the stage for the practical strategies and exercises you will introduce in the following chapters to help readers align their mind, body, and spirit for optimal health and personal growth. key points you can use to address the misconception that the body is just a machine:

Emphasize the organic complexity of the body: Explain that the body is not a simple machine with discrete, interchangeable parts. Rather, it is an incredibly complex, interconnected system with blurry boundaries between organs and tissues that serve multiple functions. This organic complexity is fundamentally different from the linear, reductionist nature of machines.

Highlight the role of natural selection: Whereas machines are designed by engineers, the human body is the product of millions of years of evolution through natural selection.

This means the body has inherent limitations and compromises that cannot simply be "redesigned from scratch" like a machine.

Discuss the limitations of the machine metaphor: Acknowledge that the machine metaphor has been useful in advancing our scientific understanding of the body, but also explain how it can distort our thinking by encouraging a view of the body as a collection of discrete, interchangeable parts that can be repaired or replaced.

Emphasize the body's self-regulating, adaptive nature: Unlike machines, the body has an incredible capacity for self-regulation, adaptation, and healing. It is not a static, lifeless object, but a dynamic, living system that responds to internal and external stimuli in complex ways.

Challenge the notion of the body as a "biochemical machine": Explain that while the body does operate on biochemical and biophysical principles, it is not merely a collection of inanimate chemical reactions. The body is a sacred temple that houses our eternal spirit and consciousness, which cannot be reduced to a purely mechanistic view.

Discuss the limitations of the "repair or replace" approach: Highlight how surgical interventions and other medical treatments aimed at "fixing" the body often fall short, as the repaired or replaced parts are never quite the same as the original. A more holistic, integrative approach is often needed to restore balance and function. By addressing these key points, you can help readers understand the profound limitations of the body-as-machine metaphor and encourage a more nuanced, holistic view of the human body as a complex, living, and sacred organism.

Chapter 2

The Power of Vision

Imagine being the CEO of your own mind, making decisions that align with your deepest desires and values. It's a powerful feeling, isn't it? To live a life that is truly yours, where every step you take is guided by a clear sense of purpose. That's what I want to help you achieve today.

As a CEO, you know that setting a clear vision for your company is crucial for success. It gives your team direction, motivation, and a sense of unity Similarly, defining your vision for your life is essential for living a fulfilling and meaningful existence. When you have a clear purpose, you can focus your energies on what truly matters, making every moment count.

Discover Your Passion

To define your vision, you need to tap into your deepest passions and desires. What gets you excited? What do you love doing? What problems do you want to solve? Take some time to reflect on these questions, and you'll start to uncover the threads that weave together to form your unique vision.

Make It Specific

Now that you have a sense of what drives you, it's time to make your vision specific. What does your ideal life look like? What are your goals, and how will you achieve them? Write down your vision in a way that is both inspiring and achievable. This will be your roadmap to success.

Make It Your Own

Remember, your vision is personal and unique to you. Don't compare yourself to others or try to fit into someone else's mold. Your vision should be a reflection of your values, passions, and strengths. Embrace your individuality and let your vision shine!

Take Action

Now that you have a clear vision, it's time to take action. Break down your goals into smaller, manageable steps, and start working towards them. Celebrate your successes and learn from your setbacks. With each step, you'll be closer to living the life you truly want.

Within Conclusion

Defining your vision is the first step towards becoming the CEO of your mind. It is a powerful tool that will guide you towards your dreams and help you live a life that is truly yours. So, take the time to reflect on your passions, make your vision specific, and take action towards making it a reality. You got this!

Next Steps

Reflect on Your Passions: Take some time to think about what truly drives you and what you love doing.

Make Your Vision Specific: Write down your ideal life and the steps you'll take to achieve it.

Define Your Vision: Establish a clear purpose for your life, just like a CEO sets a vision for their company. This gives your actions direction and meaning.

Take Action: Once your vision is established, take concrete steps to achieve it. This includes setting goals and making adjustments as needed.

Audit Your Life: Regularly evaluate all aspects of your life, including relationships, to ensure they align with your vision.

Surround yourself with positive influences and minimize negative ones.

Manage Your Workflow: Use tools like journaling and goal-setting to stay organized and focused on your objectives. Practice Mindfulness: Live in the present moment, free from distractions and negative thoughts. This helps you stay centered, calm, and focused on your goals.

Learn from Mistakes: View mistakes as opportunities for growth and learning, rather than failures. This mindset helps you adapt and improve over time.

Stay Accountable: Regularly reflect on your progress and make adjustments as needed. This ensures you stay on track and make the most of your time. By following these steps,you can effectively manage your mind and live the life you want with ease. The key is to create a visual representation of your ideal self and lifestyle. This can help program your subconscious mind, foster positive thinking, and provide clarity to achieve your personal growth aspirations. Benefits of using a dream board for mental health . Using a dream board can have numerous benefits for mental clarity:

Clarifies Goals: Creating a dream board helps you articulate your aspirations with precision, providing a clear roadmap for focused action.

Boosts Creativity: Engaging in creative activities like vision boards can enhance your mental well-being by providing an outlet for emotional expression and stress relief.

Increases Positivity: Regularly viewing your dream board can reinforce positive affirmations and beliefs in your ability to achieve your goals, fostering a resilient mindset.

Enhances Self-Efficacy: Building a vision board reinforces the belief that your goals are attainable, boosting self-efficacy and motivation to achieve them.

Provides Motivation: Having a visual representation of your goals can motivate you to work towards them, especially during times of low motivation.

Destresses: The creative process of creating a vision board can be cathartic, offering moments of respite from daily stressors and pressures.

Increases Emotional Connection: The personal significance of the images and symbols on your board infuses your goals with deeper meaning and passion, driving sustained motivation and well-being.

Helps with Goal Setting: Vision boards can help you clarify and refine your goals, making them more specific and achievable.

Increases Awareness: Reflecting on your vision board can reveal insights into your hopes, goals, and dreams, helping you make more informed choices about your life.

Enhances Focus: Having a visual reminder of your goals can help you stay focused and maintain a positive attitude, even in the face of challenges.

By incorporating a dream board into your mental health journey, you can harness the power of visualization, emotional connection, and positive reinforcement to achieve a more resilient and fulfilling life.

Here's a step-by-step guide to creating a dream board for personal development:

Step 1: Define Your Vision: Identify areas you want to improve or change in your life. Ask yourself powerful questions to gain clarity on your goals and aspirations.

Step 2: Gather Materials

Magazines (various topics)

- ☐ Scissors

☐ Glue or a glue stick

☐ A large piece of cardboard, foam board,

or poster board

☐ Markers or colored pencils

☐ Printed quotes or phrases that inspire you.

☐ **Step 3: Create Your Collage**

☐ Flip through the magazines and cut out

☐ images that resonate with your goals

and aspirations.

☐ Arrange the images on your board in a

way that is visually appealing and

meaningful to you.

☐ Add quotes or phrases that inspire you

to your board.Use markers or colored pencils to add color and

texture.

Step 4: Add Personal Touches

Include personal symbols or objects that hold significance for

you.

1. Write down affirmations or motivational phrases to
   reinforce your goals.

2. Add a personal message or mantra to your board.

Step 5: Display Your Board

1. Place your dream board in a prominent location where you will see it regularly.

2. Make it a habit to regularly review and reflect on your board.

Example: Dream Board for Personal Development

Goal: Main is, to become a registered nurse.

Images: A picture of a nurse in a hospital setting.

☐ A medical symbol or logo.

☐ A photo of a person receiving care or support.

☐ **Quotes:** "Empathy is the foundation of nursing." "Compassion is the highest form of intelligence."

☐ **Personal Touches:** Add small stuffed animal representing a patient.

☐ **A handwritten note:** With the phrase "I am capable and compassionate".

☐ **Tips and Variations:** Create a digital dream board using a tool like Canva, or Google Docs.

☐ Involve friends or family members in the

creation process for added support and

motivation.

☐ Update your board regularly to

reflect changes in your goals and aspirations.

☐ Use different colors or themes to represent

different areas of your life (e.g., career,

relationships, health). By following these steps and incorporating your personal goals and aspirations, you can create a dream board that serves as a powerful tool for personal development and mental clarity.

Here are the key steps to align a dream board with long-term goals:

Define SMART Goals: Start by setting specific, measurable, achievable, relevant, and time-bound (SMART) goals for your long-term vision. This provides a clear roadmap for your dream board.

Collect Relevant Visuals: Gather images, words, and symbols that directly represent your SMART goals and the lifestyle you want to achieve. Avoid including unrelated elements.

Arrange the Board Intentionally: Organize your dream board in a way that visually depicts the hierarchy and timeline of your

SMART goals. Group related elements together.

Break Down Goals into Actions: For each long-term goal, identify the smaller, actionable steps needed to achieve it. Incorporate these into your dream board through notes, timelines, or additional visuals.

- ☐ **Track Progress Regularly:** Frequently review your dream board and assess your progress against your SMART goals. Celebrate milestones and make adjustments as needed.
- ☐ **Maintain Alignment:** Ensure your dream board continues to accurately reflect your evolving long-term goals and vision. Update it as your priorities or circumstances change.

The key is to create a dream board that is tightly aligned with your specific, measurable, and time-bound long-term goals. This will help you stay focused, motivated, and on track to achieve your desired outcomes.

- ☐ **How to regularly:** You can update a vision board

  Steps to regularly update your vision board

- ☐ **Set a Schedule:** Decide on a specific time, such as your birthday, the new year, or the start of a new season, to review and revise your vision board.

- ☐ **Create in a Positive Mindset:** Ensure you update your vision board in a relaxed, positive mood to reflect your true desires and avoid fears or doubts.

- ☐ **Find a Quiet Space:** Choose a comfortable, distraction-free environment to work on your vision board updates.

- ☐ **Gather Necessary Materials:** Assemble the materials you need, such as magazines, newspapers, photos, scissors, glue, and markers.

- ☐ **Celebrate Achievements:** Acknowledge and celebrate the goals you have achieved by marking them off or adding visual indicators to your board.

- ☐ **Adjust Goals as Needed:** Remove or replace images and words that no longer align with your current goals and aspirations.

- ☐ **Incorporate New Inspirations:** Add new images, words, and symbols that represent your evolving dreams and objectives.

- ☐ **Maintain Alignment:** Ensure your vision board continues to accurately reflect your long-term vision and SMART goals.

- [ ] **Display Prominently:** Place your updated vision board in a visible location where you can regularly see and interact with it.

The key is to approach the updating process with intention, positivity, and a willingness to adapt to the changes in your life. Regularly refreshing your vision board can help you stay focused, motivated, and on track to achieve your personal development goals.

How to celebrate achievements on a vision board To celebrate achievements on a vision board, follow these steps:

Mark Off Achievements: Use a sticker, marker, or pin to indicate that you have completed a goal. This visual representation helps you acknowledge and celebrate your successes.

- [ ] **Add Photos or Notes:** Include a photo or note that shows your result or feeling.

- [ ] For example, if you ran a marathon, add a picture of yourself crossing the finish line or a note that says "I did it!".

- [ ] **Reflect and Rejoice:** Take a moment to reflect on your achievement and how it aligns with your vision board goals.

- [ ] Celebrate your success by acknowledging your hard work and progress.
- [ ] **Keep a Visual Journal:** Keep a visual journal to track your progress and note any signs that you are moving towards your dreams. This helps you stay motivated and focused on your goals.
- [ ] **Adjust and Refine:** After celebrating your achievements, review your vision board to adjust and refine your goals as needed. This ensures your board remains aligned with your evolving aspirations. By following these steps, you can effectively celebrate your achievements on a vision board, boosting your confidence, happiness, and motivation to continue working towards your goals.

Creative ways to mark achievements on a vision board: Ways to mark achievements on your vision board:

- [ ] **Stickers or Stamps:** Use colorful stickers or stamps to place a visual indicator next to the goals or images you have accomplished. This provides a satisfying way to celebrate your progress.
- [ ] **Handwritten Notes:** Write a brief note or message next to the relevant image or goal, expressing your feelings of accomplishment and pride.
- [ ] **Pins or Pushpins:** Attach small pins or pushpins to the

areas of your vision board that represent completed objectives. This creates a tactile way to mark your achievements.

- ☐ **Highlighters or Markers:** Use highlighters or colored markers to draw a border, circle, or checkmark around the goals you have achieved. This makes them stand out visually.

- ☐ **Photos or Mementos:** Incorporate photos, ticket stubs, or other physical mementos that represent your accomplishments and attach them to your vision board.

- ☐ **Digital Annotations:** If you have a digital vision board, use the app or software annotation tools to add text, emojis, or other digital markers to highlight your progress.

- ☐ **Journaling:** Keep a written record of your achievements in a journal that you can reference alongside your vision board. This provides additional context and reflection.

- ☐ **Themed Sections:** Dedicate specific areas of your vision board to completed goals, allowing you to visually track your overall progress. The key is to choose methods that are meaningful and visually appealing to you, making the process of celebrating your achievements an integral part of your vision board experience.

- ☐ **Ribbon or String:** Use a ribbon or string to create a visual connection between the goals you have achieved. This can be a creative way to represent the progress you have made. **Stamps or Stencils:** Use stamps or stencils with motivational messages or symbols to add a personal touch to your vision board. This can help reinforce positive affirmations and self-confidence.

- ☐ **Collage Elements:** Incorporate collage elements, such as cut-out words or images, to create a visually appealing representation of your achievements. This can be a fun and creative way to celebrate your successes.

- ☐ Digital Icons: Use digital icons or emojis to mark your achievements on a digital vision board. This can be a quick and easy way to visually represent your progress.

- ☐ **Personal Symbols:** Incorporate personal symbols or objects that hold significance for you, such as a favorite quote or a meaningful trinket.

This can make the process of celebrating your achievements more personal and meaningful.

☐ **Color-Coding:** Use different colors to categorize and highlight your achievements.

For example, you can use green for completed goals and red for ongoing projects.

☐ **Storytelling:** Write a brief story or description next to the goals you have achieved, highlighting the challenges you faced and the lessons you learned. This can help you reflect on your progress and stay motivated. By incorporating these creative methods into your vision board, you can make the process of celebrating your achievements more engaging, enjoyable, and meaningful.

Chapter 3

The Cognitive Landscape - Understanding the Terrain of Your Mind

The cognitive landscape is a vast and intricate terrain that governs our thoughts, emotions, and beliefs. It is the foundation upon which we build our perceptions, make decisions, and navigate the world around us. In this chapter, we will delve into the workings of this landscape and explore why cultivating it is crucial for personal growth, emotional well-being, and effective communication.

The Cognitive Landscape: A Complex Ecosystem

Imagine your mind as a vast, ever-changing landscape. This landscape comprises various features, including thoughts, emotions, beliefs, and memories. Each of these elements interacts with the others, influencing the overall topography of your mind. Just as a landscape can be shaped by natural forces like wind and water, your cognitive landscape is influenced by your experiences, environment, and the people around you. The Importance of Understanding your Cognitive Landscape Cultivating your cognitive landscape is vital for several reasons:

Improved Self-Awareness: By understanding your thoughts, emotions, and beliefs, you can gain a deeper understanding of yourself and your motivations. This self-awareness enables you to make more informed decisions and navigate challenging situations more effectively.

Enhanced Emotional Regulation: Recognizing the emotional terrain of your mind allows you to better manage your emotions, reducing stress and anxiety. This, in turn, fosters a sense of emotional well-being and resilience.

Effective Communication: By understanding your own cognitive landscape, you can better communicate with others, as you will be more aware of your own biases and emotional triggers. This leads to more empathetic and productive interactions.

Personal Growth: Exploring and understanding your cognitive landscape enables you to identify areas for personal growth and development. By acknowledging and addressing these areas, you can cultivate a more positive and fulfilling life.

The Journey Begins: Exploring Your Cognitive Landscape In the following chapters, we will embark on a practical journey to explore and understand your cognitive landscape. We will delve into the world of thoughts, emotions, and beliefs, and provide you with tools and techniques to cultivate a deeper understanding of yourself. This journey will be both personal and transformative, as you gain insight into the workings of your mind and develop the skills to navigate its complexities.

Within Conclusion

The cognitive landscape is a rich and dynamic terrain that holds the key to personal growth, emotional well-being, and effective communication. By understanding and cultivating this landscape, you can unlock the full potential of your mind and live a more fulfilling life. In the next chapter, we will explore the world of thoughts, the foundation of your cognitive landscape, and begin our practical journey to self-discovery.

Navigating the Realm of Thoughts

In the previous chapter, we explored the concept of the cognitive landscape and its importance in personal growth and self-understanding. Now, we delve deeper into the realm of thoughts, the fundamental building blocks of this landscape.

The Nature of Thoughts

Thoughts are the constant stream of mental processes that flow through our minds, shaping our perceptions, influencing our emotions, and guiding our actions. They can be positive, negative, rational, or irrational, and they can arise spontaneously or as a result of conscious deliberation. Understanding the nature of your thoughts is crucial, as they form the foundation of your cognitive landscape. By becoming aware of your thought patterns, you can begin to recognize and challenge the beliefs and assumptions that underlie them.

The Power of Thought Awareness

Cultivating thought awareness: Is a powerful tool for personal growth and self-improvement. When you become more attuned to your thought processes, you can:

Identify Unhelpful Thought Patterns: By recognizing negative or irrational thought patterns, you can work to replace them with more constructive and empowering ones.

Enhance Decision-Making: With a deeper understanding of your thought processes, you can make more informed and intentional decisions, leading to better outcomes.

Manage Emotions: As thoughts and emotions are closely intertwined, developing thought awareness can help you better regulate your emotional responses.

Improve Communication: By understanding your own thought patterns, you can communicate more effectively with others, as you'll be more aware of your biases and assumptions.

Practical Techniques for Thought Awareness

To cultivate thought awareness, we will explore several practical techniques:

Mindfulness Meditation

Mindfulness meditation is a powerful tool for developing present-moment awareness and observing your thoughts without judgment. By practicing mindfulness, you can learn to witness your thoughts as they arise, rather than becoming entangled in them.

Journaling: Regular journaling can help you capture and examine your thought patterns.

By writing down your thoughts, you can gain valuable insights into your cognitive landscape and identify areas for growth.

Thought-Stopping Techniques: When faced with negative or unhelpful thoughts, you can employ thought-stopping techniques, such as mental interruption or cognitive reframing, to redirect your mind towards more constructive thinking.

Cognitive Behavioral Therapy (CBT) Exercises: CBT-based exercises can help you identify and challenge the underlying beliefs and assumptions that shape your thought patterns, leading to more positive and empowering ways of thinking.

Embracing the Journey of Thought Exploration: Navigating the realm of thoughts is an ongoing journey of self-discovery and personal growth. By cultivating thought awareness, you will gain a deeper understanding of your cognitive landscape, empowering you to make more informed decisions, manage your emotions more effectively, and communicate with greater clarity and authenticity. In the next chapter, we will explore the emotional terrain of your cognitive landscape, delving into the intricate relationship between thoughts and feelings, and providing practical strategies for emotional regulation and well-being.

The Emotional Landscape: A Complex Topography The emotional landscape is a dynamic and ever-changing terrain, shaped by our thoughts, experiences, and environment. It is characterized by a vast array of emotions.

Chapter 4

The Emotional Landscape- Understanding the Terrain of Feelings

In the previous chapters, we have explored the cognitive landscape, focusing on the realm of thoughts and the importance of thought awareness. Now, we turn our attention to the emotional landscape, examining the intricate relationship between thoughts and feelings.

Emotional states to the intense and overwhelming feelings that can dominate our lives.

The Power of Emotional Awareness: Cultivating emotional awareness is essential for personal growth, emotional well-being, and effective communication.

By understanding and acknowledging your emotions, you can:

Enhance Emotional Regulation: Recognizing and accepting your emotions allows you to better manage them, reducing stress and anxiety.

Improve Relationships: Emotional awareness enables you to communicate more effectively with others, fostering deeper connections and more empathetic interactions. Increase Self-Awareness: By exploring your emotional landscape, you can gain a deeper understanding of yourself, your motivations, and your values.

Foster Resilience: Developing emotional awareness and regulation skills can help you better cope with adversity and bounce back from challenges.

The Emotional Spectrum: A Guide to Understanding Your Feelings. The emotional spectrum is a vast and diverse range of emotions, from the positive and uplifting to the negative and challenging. By understanding the different emotions that make up this spectrum, you can better navigate your emotional landscape:

Positive Emotions: Positive emotions, such as joy, gratitude, and love, are essential for emotional well-being and can have a profound impact on our mental and physical health.

Negative Emotions: Negative emotions, such as fear, anger, and sadness, can be overwhelming and debilitating if left unchecked. However, they can also serve as valuable indicators of unmet needs or unresolved issues.

Neutral Emotions: Neutral emotions, such as boredom, apathy, or indifference, can be a sign of emotional numbness or disconnection. By acknowledging and exploring these emotions, you can cultivate a deeper sense of emotional awareness. Practical Strategies for Emotional Awareness and Regulation To cultivate emotional awareness and regulation, we will explore several practical strategies:

Emotional Labeling: Labeling your emotions can help you acknowledge and accept them, reducing emotional intensity and increasing emotional regulation.

Emotional Expression: Expressing your emotions through

creative outlets, such as writing, art, or music, can provide a healthy release and help you process your emotions.

Mindfulness and Meditation: Mindfulness and meditation practices can help you develop present-moment awareness, reducing emotional reactivity and increasing emotional regulation.

Emotional Journaling: Regular journaling can help you capture and explore your emotions, gaining valuable insights into your emotional landscape and identifying areas for growth.

Embracing the Journey of Emotional Exploration: Navigating the emotional landscape is a lifelong journey of self-discovery and personal growth. By cultivating emotional awareness and regulation, you will gain a deeper understanding of yourself, your emotions, and your relationships, empowering you to live a more authentic, fulfilling, and emotionally resilient life. In the next chapter, we will explore the realm of beliefs, examining the role they play in shaping our cognitive and emotional landscapes, and providing practical strategies for challenging and reframing limiting beliefs.

Overcoming Obstacles: Strategies and Techniques to Overcome the Obstacles and Limitations that Prevent You from Growing and Prospering

For example: If you were a healthcare assistant, you were undoubtedly passionate about supporting others in their health and wellness journeys. However, you may have encountered obstacles that hinder your own growth and prosperity. This chapter aims to provide you with effective strategies and

techniques to overcome these obstacles and limitations, empowering you to achieve your career goals and personal aspirations.

Understanding Obstacles: Obstacles can be internal or external, and they often manifest in various forms, such as fear, self-doubt, lack of resources, or societal expectations. It is essential to recognize that obstacles are a natural part of the growth process, and they can be overcome with the right mindset and approach.

Strategies for Overcoming Obstacles

Identify and Acknowledge Obstacles: The first step in overcoming obstacles is to identify and acknowledge them. Take time to reflect on the challenges you face, and be honest with yourself about the obstacles that hold you back.

Reframe Negative Thoughts: Negative thoughts can be a significant obstacle to growth and prosperity. Practice reframing negative thoughts by focusing on the positive aspects of a situation and rephrasing negative self-talk.

Develop a Growth Mindset: A growth mindset is essential for overcoming obstacles. Embrace challenges as opportunities for growth and development, and believe that your abilities can be developed through dedication and hard work.

Build Resilience: Resilience is the ability to bounce back from setbacks and failures. Develop resilience by practicing self-care, setting realistic goals, and celebrating small victories.

Seek Support: Overcoming obstacles can be a solitary experience, but it does not have to be.

Seek support from colleagues, mentors, or friends who can offer guidance, encouragement, and motivation.

Practice Mindfulness: Mindfulness is the practice of being present in the moment, without judgment. Practice mindfulness to reduce stress and anxiety, and to increase your ability to focus and stay motivated.

Celebrate Small Victories: Celebrating small victories can help to build momentum and motivation. Acknowledge and celebrate your achievements, no matter how small they may seem.

Embrace Failure: Failure is an inevitable part of the growth process. Embrace failure as an opportunity to learn and grow, and use it as a stepping stone to success.

Techniques for Overcoming Obstacles

Visualization: Visualization is a powerful technique for overcoming obstacles. Close your eyes and vividly imagine yourself overcoming the obstacle, feeling confident and successful.

Positive Self-Talk: Positive self-talk is a simple yet effective technique for overcoming obstacles.

Speak positively to yourself, focusing on your strengths and abilities.

Mindfulness Meditation: Mindfulness meditation is a technique that can help to reduce stress and anxiety, and increase your ability to focus and stay motivated. Practice mindfulness meditation by focusing on your breath, and when your mind wanders, gently bring it back to the present moment.

Journaling: Journaling is a technique that can help to process emotions and gain clarity on challenges. Write down your thoughts and feelings, and reflect on the insights you gain.

Gratitude Practice: Practicing gratitude can help to shift your focus away from obstacles and towards the positive aspects of your life. Take time each day to reflect on the things you are grateful for.

Within Conclusion

Overcoming obstacles is an essential part of the growth process, and it requires a combination of strategies and techniques. By identifying and acknowledging obstacles, reframing negative thoughts, developing a growth mindset, building resilience, seeking support, practicing mindfulness, celebrating small victories, embracing failure, and using visualization, positive self-talk, mindfulness meditation, journaling, and gratitude practice, you can overcome the obstacles that prevent you from growing and prospering. Remember that overcoming obstacles is a journey, and it requires patience, persistence, and dedication With the right mindset and approach, you can achieve your career goals and personal aspirations, and live a fulfilling and successful life.

Action Plan

- ☐ Identify the obstacles that are holding you back from growing and prospering.
- ☐ Develop a plan to overcome these obstacles, using the strategies and techniques outlined in this chapter.

Practice self-care and prioritize your well-being.

- ☐ Seek support from colleagues, mentors, and friends. Celebrate small victories and milestones along the way. Embrace failure as an opportunity to learn and grow.
- ☐ Stay informed about industry trends and best practices.

Prioritize patient-centered care and stay connected with colleagues and mentors.

By following this action plan, you can overcome the obstacles that prevent you from growing and prospering, and achieve your career goals and personal goals.

Stay Positive: Maintain a positive attitude and focus on the solutions rather than the problems.

Stay Organized: Stay organized and prioritize your tasks to manage your time effectively.

Stay Focused: Stay focused on your goals and avoid distractions.

Stay Flexible: Stay flexible and adapt to changes and unexpected challenges.

Stay Connected: Stay connected with colleagues, mentors, and friends to maintain a support network.

Common Obstacles in the Healthcare Industry Communication Breakdowns:

Communication breakdowns can lead to misunderstandings

and errors. Practice effective communication and active listening.

Time Management: Poor time management can lead to burnout and decreased productivity. Prioritize tasks and manage your time effectively.

Emotional Demands: The healthcare industry can be emotionally demanding. Practice self-care and prioritize your well-being.

Limited Resources: Limited resources can be a significant obstacle to providing quality care. Seek creative solutions and collaborate with colleagues.

Societal Expectations: Societal expectations around healthcare can be challenging to navigate. Stay informed about industry trends and best practices.

Within Conclusion

Overcoming obstacles is an essential part of the growth process, and it requires a combination of strategies and techniques. By identifying and acknowledging obstacles, reframing negative thoughts, developing a growth mindset, building resilience, seeking support, practicing mindfulness, celebrating small victories, embracing failure, and using visualization, positive self-talk, mindfulness meditation, journaling, and gratitude practice, you can overcome the obstacles that prevent you from growing and prospering.

Remember that overcoming obstacles is a journey, and it requires patience, persistence, and dedication. With the right mindset and approach, you can achieve your career goals and personal aspirations, and live a fulfilling and successful life.

Action Plan

- [ ] Identify the obstacles that are holding you back from growing and prospering.
- [ ] Develop a plan to overcome these obstacles, using the strategies and techniques outlined in this chapter.
- [ ] Practice self-care and prioritize your well-being. Seek support from colleagues, mentors, and friends.
- [ ] Celebrate small victories and milestones along the way.
- [ ] Embrace failure as an opportunity to learn and grow.
- [ ] Stay informed about industry trends and best practices.
- [ ] Prioritize patient-centered care and stay connected with colleagues and mentors. By following this action plan, you can overcome the obstacles that prevent you from

growing and prospering, and achieve your career goals and personal aspirations.

Play attention to your intuition, and your common sense

Overcoming obstacles is a crucial part of personal and professional growth. By understanding the obstacles that you face, developing strategies and techniques to overcome them, and staying positive, organized, focused, flexible, and connected, you can achieve your goals and live a fulfilling and successful life. Remember to stay patient, persistent, and dedicated, and to celebrate your successes along the way.

Chapter 5

The Importance of Mindfulness: A chapter dedicated to the practice of mindfulness and its impact on mental well-being

Mindfulness is a powerful tool that has gained significant attention in recent years due to its profound impact on mental well-being. As a healthcare assistant, it is essential to understand the significance of mindfulness and how it can be incorporated into daily life to improve overall health and wellness. In this chapter, we will delve into the concept of mindfulness, its benefits, and provide practical tips on how to cultivate this practice.

What is Mindfulness?

Mindfulness is the practice of being fully present and engaged in the current moment, while cultivating a non-judgmental awareness of one's thoughts, feelings, and bodily sensations.

It involves paying attention to the present moment with openness, curiosity, and a willingness to be with what is, as it is. Mindfulness is not about achieving a specific state or outcome but rather about cultivating awareness and acceptance of the present moment.

The Benefits of Mindfulness: Research has consistently shown that mindfulness has numerous benefits for mental well-being, including:

Reduced Stress and Anxiety. Mindfulness has been shown to reduce symptoms of stress and anxiety by promoting relaxation and decreasing rumination.

Improved Emotional Regulation: Mindfulness helps individuals better manage their emotions, leading to increased emotional intelligence and resilience.

Enhanced Focus and Concentration: Mindfulness improves attention and concentration by training the mind to stay focused on the present moment.

Increased Self-Awareness: Mindfulness increases self-awareness, allowing individuals to better understand their thoughts, feelings, and behaviors.

Better Sleep: Mindfulness has been linked to improved sleep quality and duration.

Practical Tips for Cultivating Mindfulness

Start Small: Begin with short, daily mindfulness exercises, such as focusing on the breath or body sensations.

Practice Regularly: Aim to practice mindfulness daily, even if it's just for a few minutes.

Use Guided Meditations

Utilize guided meditations to help you stay focused and learn various mindfulness techniques.

Incorporate Mindfulness into Daily Activities

Bring mindfulness into daily activities such as eating, walking, or showering by paying attention to the sensations and experiences.

Seek Support

Join a mindfulness group or find a mindfulness buddy to help you stay motivated and accountable.

The Science Behind Mindfulness

Mindfulness has been extensively studied in various fields, including psychology, neuroscience, and medicine. Research has shown that mindfulness can alter the structure and function of the brain, leading to changes in emotional processing, attention, and memory.

Neuroplasticity and Mindfulness

Neuroplasticity refers to the brain's ability to reorganize and adapt in response to new experiences. Mindfulness has been shown to increase neuroplasticity by promoting the growth of new neurons and forming new connections between brain cells. This can lead to improved cognitive function, emotional regulation, and memory.

The Default Mode Network

The default mode network (DMN) is a network of brain regions that are active when we are not focused on the present moment.

The DMN is responsible for rumination, worry, and mind-wandering. Mindfulness has been shown to decrease activity in the DMN, leading to reduced symptoms of depression and anxiety.

The Anterior Cingulate Cortex

The anterior cingulate cortex (ACC) is a region of the brain involved in error detection, conflict monitoring, and motivation. Mindfulness has been shown to increase activity in the ACC, leading to improved emotional regulation and decision-making.

Mindfulness and Emotional Processing

Mindfulness has been shown to alter emotional processing by increasing activity in regions involved in emotional regulation, such as the prefrontal cortex and the amygdala. This can lead to improved emotional regulation, reduced symptoms of anxiety and depression, and increased emotional intelligence.

Mindfulness and Attention

Mindfulness has been shown to improve attention by increasing activity in regions involved in attention, such as the prefrontal cortex and the parietal cortex. This can lead to improved focus, concentration, and memory.

Mindfulness and Memory

Mindfulness has been shown to improve memory by increasing activity in regions involved in memory formation, such as the hippocampus. This can lead to improved recall and retention of information.

Practical Applications of Mindfulness

Mindfulness can be applied in various settings, including: Sports and Performance: Mindfulness can be used in sports and performance settings to improve focus, concentration, and mental toughness.

Within Conclusion

Mindfulness is a powerful tool that can have a profound impact on mental well-being. By incorporating mindfulness into daily life, individuals can experience reduced stress and anxiety, improved emotional regulation, enhanced focus and concentration, increased self-awareness, and better sleep.

It is essential to understand the significance of mindfulness and how it can be incorporated into daily life to improve overall health and wellness. By following the practical tips outlined in this chapter, you can begin to cultivate mindfulness and experience its numerous benefits firsthand. Research has shown that mindfulness can alter the structure and function of the brain, leading to changes in emotional processing, attention, and memory.

By understanding the science behind mindfulness, we can better appreciate its potential benefits and incorporate it into our daily lives.

The Best Mindfulness Apps for Beginners:

Can be a great tool for those looking to start a mindfulness practice.

Here are some of the best mindfulness apps for beginners:

Headspace: Headspace is a popular meditation app that offers guided sessions and personalized features. It's a great choice for beginners, with a clear and gradual progression of courses and a diverse range of offerings.

Calm: Calm is another well-known meditation app that focuses on relaxation and stress relief. It offers guided and unguided meditations, sleep stories, and soothing sounds to create a personalized meditation environment.

Healthy Minds Program: Healthy Minds Program is a free meditation app developed by mindfulness research scientists at the University of Wisconsin-Madison. It offers a clear sequence of well-structured courses and customizable session lengths, making it an excellent choice for beginners.

Smiling Mind: Smiling Mind is a free meditation app designed specifically for children, teens, and young adults. It offers a lighthearted and simple interface, well-structured beginner courses, and a few extra meditations for sleep and unguided practice.

Insight Timer: Insight Timer is a free meditation app that offers a wide variety of guided meditations and music tracks in 44 languages. It's a great choice for beginners, with a large library of content and a user-friendly interface.

Choosing the Right App for You

When choosing a mindfulness app, consider the following factors:

Goals: What do you want to achieve through meditation? Do you want to reduce stress, improve sleep, or increase focus?

Style: Do you prefer guided meditations or unguided practice? Do you like a more structured approach or a more flexible one?

Features: Do you want additional features like sleep stories, music, or journaling prompts?

Accessibility: Do you need an app with accessibility features like closed captions or audio descriptions?

The best free mindfulness apps for beginners are: Mindfulness.com: Offers over 2,000 guided meditations from world-leading teachers, personalized daily coaching videos, and a variety of meditation courses and tools. It also includes a "For You" tab that provides customized meditations based on your preferences and goals.

Smiling Mind: A not-for-profit app with hundreds of meditations organized into structured programs for stress management, sleep, and digital detox. It also includes bite-sized meditations and activities like journaling and sensory exercises.

UCLA Mindful: Developed by the Mindful Awareness Research Centre at UCLA, this app features about a dozen meditations of different types, including a "Getting Started" section for beginners.

Healthy Minds Programme: A free app that integrates neuroscience and research-based techniques with meditation training to increase overall wellbeing. It includes active meditation practices and guidance on being mindful while exercising.

Insight Timer: Offers over 80,000 free guided meditations from over 10,000 teachers on various topics, including stress, relationships, and sleep. It also includes live events and a timer for unguided meditation. These apps cater to different needs and preferences, providing a range of meditation styles, lengths, and activities to help beginners establish a mindfulness practice.

Within Conclusion : Mindfulness apps can be a great tool for beginners, offering a convenient and accessible way to start a mindfulness practice. By considering your goals, style, features, and accessibility needs, you can choose the best app for you and start your mindfulness journey. These apps cater to different needs and preferences, providing a range of meditation styles, lengths, and activities to help beginners establish a mindfulness practice.

Chapter 6

Develop Resilience - Techniques and Strategies to Overcome Life's Challenges

Resilience is the ability to withstand and recover from adversity, trauma, or stress. It is a vital component of mental well-being, enabling individuals to cope with life's challenges and bounce back from setbacks. In this chapter, we will explore techniques and strategies to develop resilience, helping you to build a stronger, more resilient mind.

What is Resilience?

Resilience is not the absence of stress or adversity, but rather the ability to adapt and thrive in the face of challenges. It involves developing coping skills, building social support networks, and cultivating a positive mindset. Resilience is not fixed and can be developed through practice, patience, and persistence.

Techniques to Develop Resilience

Mindfulness and Meditation: Mindfulness and meditation practices can help you develop a greater sense of self-awareness, allowing you to better manage stress and emotions. Regular mindfulness practice can also increase gray matter in the brain, leading to improved emotional regulation and resilience.

Positive Self-Talk: Positive self-talk is a powerful tool for building resilience. By focusing on positive affirmations and reframing negative thoughts, you can cultivate a more optimistic mindset and develop a greater sense of self-confidence.

Social Support: Social support networks are crucial for building resilience. Surround yourself with supportive friends, family, and colleagues who can offer emotional support and encouragement.

Physical Exercise: Regular physical exercise can help reduce stress and anxiety, improve mood, and increase resilience. Exercise also releases endorphins, which can help alleviate symptoms of depression.

Gratitude Practice: Practicing gratitude can help shift your focus away from negative thoughts and cultivate a more positive mindset. Take time each day to reflect on the things you are grateful for. If you believe in God, just tell him how you feel, and what you would like to change or do.

Reframe Negative Thoughts: Reframing negative thoughts is a powerful technique for building resilience. By challenging negative self-talk and reframing negative thoughts, you can develop a more optimistic mindset and improve emotional regulation.

Take Breaks and Practice Self-Care: Taking breaks and practicing self-care is essential for building resilience. Make time for activities that bring you joy and help you relax, such as reading, taking a bath, or spending time in nature.

Seek Professional Help: If you are struggling to cope with stress, anxiety, or depression, seek professional help. A mental health professional can provide you with personalized support and guidance to help you build resilience.

Here are some techniques to build resilience in daily life:

Nurture Strong Relationships: Build and maintain good relationships with family, friends, with God, and colleagues.

This support network can help you cope with stress and adversity.

Prioritize Physical Health: Regular exercise and healthy eating can improve your mental well-being and increase resilience.

Discover Your Purpose: Having a sense of purpose can give you direction and motivation, especially during tough times. Remember that God is always there waiting to hear from you.

Embrace Change: Accept and adapt to change, which can make you more resilient and flexible.

Build Self-Confidence: Confidence in your abilities can help you face challenges more effectively.

Strategies to Overcome Life's Challenges

Break Down Challenges into Smaller Tasks: Breaking down challenges into smaller tasks can help make them feel less overwhelming and more manageable. Focus on the Present Moment: Focus on the present moment and what you can control. Avoid worrying about the future or dwelling on the past.

Practice Self-Compassion: Practice self-compassion and treat yourself with kindness and understanding. Avoid self-criticism and negative self-talk.

Seek Support from Others: Seek support from others, whether it be friends, family, or a mental health professional. Sharing your feelings and experiences with others can help you feel less isolated and more supported.

Take Care of Your Physical Health: Take care of your physical health by getting regular exercise, eating a balanced diet, and getting enough sleep. A healthy body and mind are essential for building resilience.

Reframe Negative Thoughts: Challenge negative self-talk and reframe negative thoughts to maintain a positive mindset.

Take Breaks and Practice Self-Care: Take time for yourself and engage in activities that bring you joy and relaxation.

Seek Professional Help: If you are struggling to cope with stress, anxiety, or depression, seek professional help from a mental health professional.

Celebrate Small Victories: Celebrate small victories and accomplishments to build confidence and motivation.

Practice Gratitude: Practice gratitude by focusing on the positive aspects of your life and expressing gratitude for what you have achieved until now. If you believe in God's word, you could have a look at these two biblical passages (Jeremiah 17: 7) and (Colossians 3:17).

Develop Emotional Intelligence: Develop emotional intelligence by recognizing and managing your emotions, empathizing with others, and building strong relationships.

Practice Self-Compassion: Practice self-compassion by treating yourself with kindness, understanding, and patience.

Develop a Growth Mindset: Develop a growth mindset by embracing challenges, learning from failures, and persisting in the face of obstacles.

Chapter 7

The Power of Imagination: Unlocking Your Path to Success

The importance of maintaining a positive and proactive mindset. Within this new chapter we will explore the transformative power of imagination and how it can be harnessed to achieve your personal and professional goals. Imagination is the cornerstone of human progress. It is the faculty that allows us to envision a future beyond our current circumstances, to dream of possibilities that have yet to be realized. Through the power of imagination, you can tap into your creative potential, overcome obstacles, and manifest the life you desire.

Unleashing the Synthetic and Creative Imagination

The imaginative faculty operates in two distinct forms: synthetic imagination and creative imagination. Synthetic imagination allows you to combine existing ideas, concepts, and experiences in novel ways, fueling innovation and problem-solving. Creative imagination, on the other hand, grants you direct access to infinite intelligence, enabling you to receive "hunches" and "inspirations" that can lead to groundbreaking discoveries. By actively engaging both forms of imagination, you can harness the full power of this remarkable faculty. Through regular practice and repetition, you can strengthen your imaginative muscles, becoming more adept at visualizing your goals and manifesting them into reality.

Imagination and Goal Setting

Imagination plays a pivotal role in the goal-setting process. By vividly picturing your desired outcomes, you can create a compelling vision that ignites your motivation and guides your actions. Visualization techniques, such as crafting detailed mental images of your success, can help you overcome doubts and attract the necessary resources and opportunities to achieve your aspirations.

Cultivating a Vibrant Imagination

Developing a strong and vibrant imagination requires a multifaceted approach. Engaging in activities that stimulate your creativity, such as reading, writing, or pursuing artistic hobbies, can help nurture your imaginative faculties. Additionally, adopting a mindset that embraces curiosity, flexibility, and a willingness to explore different viewpoints can further enhance your imaginative capabilities.

Imagination and Problem-Solving

When faced with challenges, your imagination can be a powerful ally. By thinking outside the box and exploring unconventional solutions, you can tap into your creative problem-solving skills and find innovative ways to overcome obstacles. Embracing a mindset of curiosity and openness to new perspectives can further enhance your imaginative abilities, empowering you to find creative solutions to even the most complex problems.

Health and wellness can be amplified by the power of imagination.

By harnessing the transformative potential of this remarkable faculty, you can envision and manifest a future where you make a profound impact on the lives of those you serve.

Embark on this journey of self-discovery and unlock the boundless possibilities that lie within your imagination. Embrace the excitement of dreaming, the thrill of problem-solving, and the satisfaction of turning your aspirations into reality. The path to success and fulfillment begins with the power of your imagination.

Harnessing the Power of Imagination for Personal Growth: Imagination is not limited to the realm of creativity and innovation; it also plays a crucial role in personal growth and self-improvement.

By using your imagination to envision a better version of yourself, you can cultivate the mindset and skills necessary to achieve your goals.

Visualizing Success: visualization is a powerful technique that involves vividly picturing yourself achieving your goals.

This can help boost your confidence, motivation, and overall performance.

By regularly visualizing your success, you can: Enhance your focus and concentration.

Overcome self-doubt and fear: Develop a stronger sense of purpose and direction Build resilience and perseverance.

Imagining Alternative Scenarios: Imagination can also be used to explore alternative scenarios and outcomes. This can help you: Develop a more nuanced understanding of complex issues Identify potential pitfalls and develop contingency plans. Cultivate a sense of adaptability and flexibility Enhance your critical thinking and problem-solving skills.

The Role of Imagination in Overcoming Adversity: Imagination can be a powerful tool in overcoming adversity and adversity. By using your imagination to envision a better future, you can:

- Develop a sense of hope and optimism
- Cultivate resilience and perseverance
- Build a support network of like-minded individuals Enhance your ability to adapt to changing circumstances.

Within Conclusion

The power of imagination is a remarkable tool that can be harnessed to achieve success, overcome adversity and cultivate personal growth. By embracing your imagination and using it to envision a better future, you can unlock your full potential and live a more fulfilling life.

Exercises to Cultivate Your Imagination

1. **Mind Mapping:** Create a visual representation of your goals and aspirations. Use colors, symbols, and images to bring your vision to life.

2. **Visualization:** Spend 10 minutes each day visualizing yourself achieving your goals. Use vivid details and sensory experiences to bring your vision to life.

3. **Free Writing:** Write a short story or poem about your goals and aspirations. Use your imagination to explore different scenarios and outcomes.

4. **Mindfulness Meditation:** Practice mindfulness meditation to cultivate a greater sense of awareness and presence. Use this awareness to tap into your imaginative faculties and explore different scenarios and outcomes.

Resumen thoughts

You have the power to transform your life. And the lives of those you serve. By harnessing the power of your imagination, you can envision a brighter future for yourself and those around you. Remember to cultivate your imaginative faculties through regular practice and repetition. With dedication and persistence, you can unlock the full potential of your imagination and achieve your goals.

Chapter 8

The Importance of Communication

Communication is the foundation upon which we build our relationships, both personal and professional. It is the means by which we express our thoughts, feelings, and ideas, and it is essential for maintaining healthy connections with others. In this chapter, we will explore the significance of effective communication and how it can be used to enhance our relationships and mental well-being.

The Power of Effective Communication

Effective communication involves more than just conveying information; it requires active listening, empathy, and the ability to express oneself clearly and concisely. When we communicate effectively, we are able to build trust, resolve conflicts, and deepen our connections with others. By mastering the art of communication, we can unlock the potential for personal growth, professional success, and overall happiness.

Improving Relationships through Communication

Communication is the lifeblood of any relationship. Whether you are navigating a romantic partnership, nurturing a friendship, or interacting with colleagues, effective communication is key to maintaining a healthy and fulfilling connection. By actively listening to others, expressing your needs and boundaries, and practicing open and honest dialogue, you can strengthen the bonds you share and create a foundation of mutual understanding and respect.

The Link between Communication and Mental Well-being

Communication not only impacts our relationships but also plays a crucial role in our mental health. When we are able to express our thoughts and feelings openly and without fear of judgment, we can release emotional tension and gain a sense of clarity and control over our lives. Conversely, when communication breaks down or becomes strained, it can lead to feelings of isolation, anxiety, and depression. By prioritizing effective communication and seeking support when needed, we can cultivate a healthier and more balanced mental state.

Overcoming Communication Barriers

Despite the importance of communication, there are often barriers that can hinder our ability to connect effectively with others. These barriers can include cultural differences, language barriers, personal biases, and emotional baggage. By acknowledging these barriers and making a conscious effort to overcome them, we can create a more inclusive and understanding communication environment.

Within Conclusion

In conclusion, communication is a powerful tool that can transform our relationships and our mental well-being. By embracing effective communication strategies, we can build stronger connections, resolve conflicts more effectively, and cultivate a greater sense of personal fulfillment. Remember, communication is a skill that can be learned and improved upon with practice and dedication. Embrace the power of communication and unlock the door to a more connected and fulfilling life.

What are the key elements of effective communication in relationships

The key elements of effective communication in relationships include:

- **Active Listening:** Fully engaging with the other person, focusing on their words, and avoiding distractions to demonstrate that you understand their perspective.
- **Empathy:** Trying to understand the other person's feelings and emotions, and validating their experiences to create a safe space for open communication.
- **Clarity:** Expressing your thoughts and feelings clearly and concisely, using language the other person can understand. Avoiding vague or ambiguous communication.
- **Timing:** Choosing the right time and place to have important conversations, when both parties are calm and receptive.
- **Feedback:** Actively seeking and being open to feedback to improve communication and deepen the relationship.
- **Adaptability:** Tailoring your communication style to match the other person's preferences and needs.
- **Transparency:** Being open and honest, and providing relevant information to build trust and credibility.

By incorporating these key elements, you can improve the quality of your relationships and foster stronger, more fulfilling connections with others. Effective communication is essential for resolving conflicts, meeting each other's needs, and maintaining healthy, long-lasting relationships.

Mastering the Art of Effective Communication in Relationships

Active Listening: The Foundation of Mutual Understanding

At the heart of effective communication lies the ability to truly listen. Active listening involves fully engaging with the speaker, focusing your attention on their words, tone, and body language, and seeking to understand their perspective without interruption or judgment. By demonstrating that you have heard and comprehended the other person's message, you create a safe and supportive environment for open dialogue.

Empathy: It goes beyond just exchanging information; It requires the ability to empathize with the other person. Connecting on an Emotional Level. Effective communication of a person's feelings and experiences. When you approach a conversation with empathy, you are able to validate the other person's emotions, offer emotional support, and foster a deeper sense of connection and understanding.

Feedback and Adaptability: Continuously Improving Effective communication is an ongoing process that requires continuous feedback and adaptation. Be open to receiving constructive feedback from your conversation partner, and be willing to adjust your communication style to better meet their needs. By embracing a growth mindset, you can continuously improve your communication skills and deepen the connections in your relationships.

Clarity and Concision

Expressing Yourself Effectively Clear and concise communication is essential for ensuring that your message is understood and received as intended. Avoid using jargon, vague language, or overly complex sentences. Instead, strive to express your thoughts and feelings in a straightforward and easily digestible manner, tailoring your communication style to the needs and preferences of your conversation partner. Timing and Context: Choosing the Right Moment The timing and context of a conversation can greatly impact its effectiveness. Choose a time and place where both you and the other person are calm, focused, and receptive to open communication. Avoid having important discussions when emotions are running high or when there are distractions or time constraints.

Transparency and Trust

Building a Foundation of Honesty Effective communication is built on a foundation of trust and transparency. By being open and honest in your communication, you demonstrate your commitment to the relationship and create an environment where both parties feel safe to express their thoughts and feelings without fear of judgment or repercussion.

Within Conclusion

Unlocking the Power of Effective Communication. Mastering the art of effective communication is a journey, but the rewards are immeasurable. By incorporating these key elements into your relationships, you can build stronger, more fulfilling connections, resolve conflicts more effectively, and cultivate a greater sense of personal well-being. Embrace the power of communication and unlock the door to a more connected and meaningful life.

What role does body language play in effective communication

Body language plays a crucial role in effective communication for several key reasons:

1. **Enhanced Understanding:** Body language provides more accurate insights into a person's emotions, intentions, and underlying feelings than just their words alone. Reading body language cues can lead to better comprehension and deeper connections between communicators.

2. **Conveying Emotions:** Facial expressions, and posture can convey emotions with precision, helping to express feelings like happiness, sadness, anger, or empathy more effectively. This allows for a more nuanced understanding of others' emotional states.

3. **Building Trust:** Positive body language, such as maintaining eye contact and open posture, fosters trust, rapport, and credibility between communicators. This lays the foundation for meaningful connections.

4. **Conflict Resolution:** The ability to read subtle body language cues can aid in detecting underlying tensions or misunderstandings, facilitating conflict resolution and promoting harmony.

Adjusting one's own body language can also signal a willingness to listen and find common ground.

5. **Complementing Verbal Communication:** Body language can enhance and complement verbal communication, providing additional context and clarity. For example, gesturing or pointing can make verbal directions more specific and helpful.

How can I improve my body language skills

Here are some key tips to improve your body language skills:

1. **Maintain Good Posture**: Stand or sit up straight with your shoulders back. Avoid slouching or crossing your arms, as this can make you appear closed off or uninterested. Good posture conveys confidence and engagement.

2. **Make Eye Contact**: Maintain appropriate eye contact when conversing with others. Look them in the eye to show you are listening and interested in what they are saying. Use the 50/70 rule - make eye contact 50% of the time when speaking and 70% when listening.

3. **Use Open Gestures**: Use open hand gestures and avoid crossing your arms. Open gestures make you appear more approachable and receptive.

4. **Smile and Nod**: Smile genuinely to project warmth and friendliness.

Nod occasionally to show you are listening and engaged in the conversation.

5. **Mirror and Match**: Subtly mirror the body language of the person you are talking to.
This helps build rapport and makes the other person feel more comfortable.

6. **Practice Self-Awareness**: Pay attention to your own body language in different situations. Notice what you do with your hands, arms, legs, and face. Video yourself to identify areas for improvement.

7. **Seek Feedback**: Ask trusted friends or colleagues for honest feedback on your body language. Their observations can help you pinpoint strengths and weaknesses.

8. **Develop Active Listening Skills**: Effective body language involves not just how you present yourself, but how you respond to others. Practice active listening by maintaining eye contact, nodding, and asking thoughtful questions.

By consistently practicing these techniques and developing self-awareness, you can significantly improve your body language skills and become a more effective communicator in both personal and professional settings.

What are some common body language habits to be aware of

Based on the search results, here are some common body language habits to be aware of:

1. **Nervous Hand Gestures:** Fidgeting, playing with hair, or keeping hands in pockets can make you appear nervous and uncomfortable.

2. **Crossed Arms:** Crossing your arms creates a physical barrier and can make you seem defensive, closed-off, or disinterested.

3. **Avoiding Eye Contact:** Avoiding eye contact can make you appear dishonest, unengaged, or arrogant. Maintaining appropriate eye contact is important.

4. **Poor Posture:** Slouching, hunching, or having a closed-off body position can make you seem timid, unconfident, or disinterested.

5. **Finger Pointing:** Pointing your finger at someone can come across as aggressive or accusatory, even if unintentional. 6. Facial Expressions: Excessive eye-rolling, raised eyebrows, or a deadpan expression can make you seem arrogant, disengaged, or unapproachable.

7. **Fidgeting:** Nervous habits like nail-biting, foot-tapping, or excessive movement can distract from your message and make you appear anxious.

8. **Defensive Positioning:** Crossing your arms, leaning away, or turning your body away from someone can signal that you are feeling defensive or closed-off. Being mindful of these common body language habits and making an effort to adopt more open, confident, and engaged body language can significantly improve your communication and interpersonal skills.

Techniques for improving posture and confidence
Here are some key techniques for improving your posture and boosting confidence:

- Posture Exercises and Stretches.

- Practice yoga poses like child's pose, standing forward fold, and cat-cow to stretch and lengthen the spine.

- Do glute bridges to strengthen your glutes and relieve lower back pain.

- Perform isometric pulls to work your shoulder, arm, and back muscles for better posture.

- Regularly exercise to improve overall posture.

Strength training, flexibility exercises, and activities like yoga and Pilates are especially helpful.

Assertive Body Language

- Stand with your feet shoulder-width apart, weight evenly distributed, and feet angled slightly outward. This assertive posture projects confidence.

- When sitting, keep your back straight with your rear against the chair back. Plant your feet firmly on the floor.

- Use open hand gestures and avoid crossing your arms, which can make you appear closed off.

- Maintain appropriate eye contact to convey honesty, approachability and confidence.

Mindset and Presence

- Avoid trying too hard to "correct" your posture, as this can look unnatural. Make subtle adjustments instead.

- Slow down your speech and allow yourself moments to breathe. Rushing can lead to tension.

- Be present with yourself and your surroundings. Poor posture often creeps in when we're distracted or focused on a task]. - Take time to reset your posture by doing a quick stretch or body scan. This can help you feel more calm and centered.

Power Posing

- Strike a powerful pose like reaching your hands in the air and standing with your feet wide apart for 2 minutes. This can boost confidence by increasing testosterone and decreasing cortisol]. - When closing a deal, place both hands on the table and lean forward to show engagement. This dominant position can help you command the room.

- Before a presentation, do a quick power pose to feel more confident and in control. By consistently practicing these posture exercises, body language techniques, and mindset shifts, you can improve your posture and project greater confidence in all areas of life. Remember, small changes add up over time.

Mastering the Art of Confident Body Language Posture

The Foundation of Confident Presence Good posture is the foundation of confident body language. By standing tall with your shoulders back and head held high, you project an aura of self-assurance and command attention. Avoid slouching or hunching, as this can make you appear timid or uninterested. Instead, practice keeping your spine straight and your weight evenly distributed on both feet.

Regular stretching and exercises that target the core, back, and shoulder muscles can help improve your posture over time.

Eye Contact: The Window to Confidence

Making eye contact is a powerful tool for projecting confidence. When you look someone directly in the eye, you convey a sense of honesty, engagement, and self-assurance. However, it's important to strike a balance – too much eye contact can be perceived as aggressive or intimidating, while too little can make you seem untrustworthy or disinterested.

Aim for maintaining eye contact for about 50% of the time when speaking and 70% when listening.

Gestures and Movement: Expressing Confidence Through Action

The way you move and gesture can have a significant impact on how confident you appear. Avoid fidgeting or keeping your hands in your pockets, as this can make you seem nervous or uncomfortable. Instead, use open hand gestures and keep your movements purposeful and controlled. When walking, maintain a steady pace and avoid shuffling or dragging your feet. If you're seated, avoid crossing your arms or legs, as this can create a physical barrier and make you seem closed off.

Facial Expressions: Conveying Confidence Through Your Face

Your facial expressions can also contribute to your overall confidence.

Avoid frowning, scowling, or looking worried

as this can make you appear anxious or unsure of yourself. Instead, practice smiling genuinely and keeping your expression relaxed and open. Raise your eyebrows slightly to create an alert, engaged expression, and avoid excessive eye-rolling or raised eyebrows, which can come across as arrogant or dismissive.

Vocal Confidence

Projecting Confidence Through Your Voice

Your voice can also play a significant role in how confident you appear. Speak clearly and confidently, avoiding mumbling or speaking too softly. Maintain a steady pace and avoid rushing your words, as this can make you seem nervous or unsure. If you're feeling anxious, take a deep breath before speaking to help calm your nerves and project a more confident tone.

Putting It All Together

Integrating Confident Body Language into Your Life

Mastering confident body language takes practice, but the rewards are well worth the effort. By consistently practicing good posture, making eye contact, using open gestures, and maintaining a relaxed, engaged facial expression, you can project an aura of confidence that will serve you well in all areas of your life. Remember, confidence is not just about how you look – it's also about how you feel. By working on your inner confidence and self-belief, you can create a powerful synergy between your thoughts, feelings, and actions that will help you achieve your goals and live your best life.

Within summary

Body language is a powerful non-verbal communication tool that can significantly improve the effectiveness of our interactions by enhancing understanding, conveying emotions, building trust, resolving conflicts, and complementing our spoken words. Mastering body language is crucial for developing strong communication skills.

Chapter 9

The Culture of Compassion

In a world that often prioritizes individualism and competition, it is easy to lose sight of the fundamental human need for connection, understanding, and support. However, by cultivating a culture of compassion and empathy, we can create a society that is more caring, inclusive, and fulfilling for all. In this chapter, we will explore the importance of compassion and empathy, and discuss practical strategies for incorporating these values into our daily lives and communities.

The Power of Compassion

Compassion is the ability to recognize and respond to the suffering of others with a genuine desire to alleviate their pain. It is a powerful force that can transform lives, heal relationships, and create a more just and equitable world.

When we approach others with compassion, we acknowledge their inherent worth and dignity, and commit to supporting them in their struggles. By practicing compassion, we not only improve the lives of those around us, but we also enhance our own well-being and sense of purpose.

The Role of Empathy

Empathy, on the other hand, is the ability to understand and share the feelings of another person. It is the foundation upon which compassion is built, as it allows us to connect with others on a deep emotional level. By cultivating empathy, we can develop a greater appreciation for the diverse experiences and perspectives of those around us, and foster a more inclusive and understanding society. Through empathy, we can break down barriers, challenge stereotypes, and build bridges between individuals and communities.

Compassion in Action

Compassion is not just a feeling, but a call to action. By engaging in compassionate behaviors, we can make a tangible difference in the lives of others and contribute to the creation of a more caring and equitable world. This can take many forms, from volunteering with local organizations, to supporting social justice causes, to simply being kind and understanding in our daily interactions.

When we put compassion into practice, we not only help others, but we also inspire those around us to do the same, creating a ripple effect of positive change.

Overcoming Barriers to Compassion

Despite the many benefits of compassion and empathy, there are often barriers that prevent us from fully embracing these values. These can include fear, prejudice, lack of understanding, or simply the demands of daily life. However, by acknowledging these barriers and making a conscious effort to overcome them, we can cultivate a more compassionate mindset and create a society that is more inclusive and supportive for all. This may involve challenging our own biases, seeking out opportunities for cross-cultural exchange, or simply taking the time to listen to and understand the experiences of others.

The Importance of Self-Compassion

Finally, it is important to recognize that compassion begins with ourselves. By practicing self-compassion, we can develop a kinder, gentler relationship with ourselves, and create a foundation of inner strength and resilience that allows us to extend compassion to others. Self-compassion involves treating ourselves with the same kindness and understanding that we would offer to a dear friend, and recognizing that our struggles and failures are a natural part of the human experience. By embracing self-compassion, we can break free from the cycle of self-criticism and shame, and cultivate a more positive and fulfilling relationship with ourselves and the world around us.

Within conclusion

The cultivation of compassion and empathy is essential for creating a more just, equitable, and fulfilling world. By embracing these values and putting them into practice in our daily lives, we can build stronger connections, foster greater understanding, and contribute to the creation of a society that values the inherent worth and dignity of all people. Through compassion, we can heal wounds, bridge divides, and create a world that is more caring, inclusive, and supportive for all. Let us embrace the power of compassion and empathy, and work together to build a culture that celebrates our shared humanity and the beauty of our diversity.

Cultivating a Compassionate Mindset Practicing Mindfulness and Presence: One of the key foundations of compassion is the ability to be fully present and attentive to the experiences of others. Mindfulness, the practice of focusing one's awareness on the present moment, can help us develop a greater sensitivity to the needs and emotions of those around us. By cultivating mindfulness through meditation, deep breathing exercises, or simply taking moments throughout the day to pause and observe our surroundings, we can become more attuned to the subtle cues and expressions that signal when someone is in need of support or understanding.

Challenging Biases and Assumptions

Another important aspect of cultivating a compassionate mindset is the willingness to challenge our own biases and assumptions about others. We all have preconceived notions and stereotypes that can shape our perceptions and interactions, often without our conscious awareness.

By taking the time to reflect on our own thought patterns and beliefs, and to actively seek out information and perspectives that challenge our assumptions, we can develop a more nuanced and empathetic understanding of the diverse experiences and identities that make up our communities.

Embracing Diversity and Inclusion: Compassion also requires a genuine appreciation for diversity and a commitment to creating inclusive spaces where all people feel valued and respected.

This means actively seeking out opportunities to engage with individuals and communities whose experiences and perspectives differ from our own, and creating environments where everyone feels safe to share their stories and express their authentic selves. By embracing diversity and inclusion, we can challenge the harmful narratives of "us vs. them" and build a society that celebrates the richness and complexity of human experience.

Developing Emotional Intelligence: Compassion is also closely linked to emotional intelligence, or the ability to recognize, understand, and manage our own emotions as well as those of others. By developing emotional intelligence through practices like journaling, therapy, or emotional regulation techniques, we can become more attuned to the nuances of emotional experience and better equipped to respond to the emotional needs of others with empathy and care. This can involve learning to identify and name our own feelings, to communicate them effectively, and to regulate them in healthy and constructive ways.

Cultivating Compassionate Communication: Finally, compassion requires the development of communication skills that prioritize understanding, validation, and support.

This means actively listening to others, asking thoughtful questions, and responding with empathy and care.

It also involves being willing to have difficult conversations and to engage in constructive conflict resolution when necessary. By cultivating compassionate communication skills, we can build stronger, more authentic relationships and create a culture of mutual understanding and support.

Putting Compassion into Practice

Volunteering and Community Engagement: One of the most tangible ways to put compassion into practice is through volunteering and community engagement. By donating our time and skills to organizations and causes that support those in need, we can make a direct and meaningful impact on the lives of others. This can involve anything from serving meals at a local food bank, to tutoring children in underserved communities, to advocating for social justice causes.

By engaging in these activities, we not only help others, but we also develop a deeper sense of connection and purpose within our communities.

Supporting Social Justice Causes: Compassion also requires a commitment to addressing systemic inequalities and working towards a more just and equitable society. This can involve supporting social justice causes through activism, advocacy, and financial contributions, as well as using our privilege and influence to challenge oppressive systems and structures. By engaging in this work, we can help to create a world where everyone has access to the resources and opportunities they need to thrive.

Practicing Kindness and Empathy in Daily Life: Finally, compassion can be practiced in the small, everyday moments that make up our lives. By offering a kind word or gesture to a stranger, by listening with an open heart to a friend in need, or by extending patience and understanding to a colleague or family member, we can make a profound difference in the lives of others. These small acts of kindness and empathy, when multiplied across communities and societies, have the power to create a culture of compassion that is both sustaining and transformative.

Within conclusion

The cultivation of compassion and empathy is essential for creating a more just, equitable, and fulfilling world. By embracing these values and putting them into practice in our daily lives, we can build stronger connections, foster greater understanding, and contribute to the creation of a society that values the inherent worth and dignity of all people. Through compassion, we can heal wounds, bridge divides, and create a world that is more caring, inclusive, and supportive for all. Let us embrace the power of compassion and empathy, and work together to build a culture that celebrates our shared humanity and the beauty of our diversity.

The Ripple Effect of Compassion

Compassion as a Catalyst for Change: When we embrace compassion as a way of being, it has the power to catalyze positive change not only in our own lives, but in the lives of those around us and in the world at large. By modeling compassionate behavior and sharing our stories of how compassion has transformed us, we can inspire others to follow suit.

This ripple effect of compassion can create a groundswell of positive change that challenges the status quo and pushes us to build a more just, equitable, and caring society.

The Healing Power of Compassion: Compassion also has the power to heal wounds, both individual and collective. When we approach those who have experienced trauma, oppression, or loss with empathy and understanding, we create a safe space for healing and growth. This healing process can take many forms, from providing emotional support and validation, to advocating for the rights and needs of marginalized communities, to working towards reconciliation and restorative justice. By harnessing the healing power of compassion, we can help to break cycles of harm and build a more resilient and connected world.

Compassion as a Pathway to Peace: At its core, compassion is a commitment to non-violence and a rejection of the use of force or coercion to resolve conflicts. When we approach disagreements and disputes with a compassionate mindset, we seek to understand the underlying needs and concerns of all parties involved and to find mutually beneficial solutions. This approach to conflict resolution, rooted in empathy and care, has the power to transform even the most intractable conflicts and to create pathways to lasting peace.

By embracing compassion as a way of being, we can help to build a world where violence and oppression are no longer seen as viable solutions to human problems.

Compassion and the Environment

Finally, compassion also extends to our relationship with the natural world and all living beings.

By cultivating a sense of kinship and stewardship towards the environment and the other species with whom we share this planet, we can work towards a more sustainable and harmonious future. This can involve making eco-friendly lifestyle choices, supporting conservation efforts, and advocating for policies that protect the rights and well-being of animals and ecosystems.

By embracing compassion as a guiding principle in our relationship with the natural world, we can help to heal the wounds of environmental degradation and build a more resilient and thriving planet for generations to come.

Compassion as a Lifelong Journey: Ultimately, the cultivation of compassion is a lifelong journey that requires ongoing commitment, reflection, and growth. There will be times when we fall short, when our biases and fears get the better of us, or when the demands of daily life make it difficult to maintain a compassionate mindset. However, by acknowledging these challenges and recommitting ourselves to the path of compassion, we can continue to grow and evolve as compassionate beings. This journey may involve seeking out opportunities for learning and growth, such as attending workshops, reading books, or engaging in dialogue with others who share our commitment to compassion. It may also involve engaging in regular practices of self-reflection and self-care, to ensure that we are able to sustain our compassionate efforts over the long term.

Most importantly, the journey of compassion requires us to approach ourselves and others with kindness, patience, and understanding.

We are all works in progress, and by embracing our own humanity and imperfections, we can create a more forgiving and supportive environment for everyone to grow and thrive.

Within conclusion

The cultivation of compassion is not only a personal journey, but a collective one that has the power to transform our relationships, our communities, and our world. By embracing compassion as a way of being and putting it into practice in our daily lives, we can create a more just, equitable, and caring society that values the inherent worth and dignity of all people. Through compassion, we can heal wounds, bridge divides, and create a world that is more resilient, sustainable, and peaceful for all. Let us embrace this journey together, and work towards a future where compassion is not just a lofty ideal, but a lived reality that shapes the way we relate to one another and the world around us.

Chapter 10

Navigating Life's Transitions

As we journey through life, we are constantly faced with change and transition. Whether it's the end of a relationship, the loss of a job, or the onset of a new phase of life, these moments of transition can be both exciting and challenging, filled with a mix of emotions and uncertainty. However, by cultivating the tools and strategies to navigate these transitions with resilience and grace, we can not only survive but thrive in the face of change.

In this chapter, we will explore the nature of life transitions, the emotional and psychological impact they can have, and the key principles and practices that can help us navigate them with greater ease and clarity. We will delve into the importance of self-awareness, the power of social support, and the transformative potential of embracing change as an opportunity for growth and renewal. Understanding the Stages of Transition. One of the first steps in navigating life's transitions is to understand the stages of the transition process itself. According to the work of William Bridges, a renowned expert on change and transition, there are three key stages that individuals typically go through when faced with a major life transition:

1.**Ending, Losing, Letting Go**: This stage involves acknowledging and grieving the loss of what was, whether it's a relationship, a job, or a way of life. It's a time of uncertainty and disorientation, as we let go of the familiar and prepare to move forward.

2. **The Neutral Zone**: This is the in-between space, where the old is gone but the new has not yet taken shape. It can be a time of confusion, anxiety, and self-doubt, but it's also a space of creativity and possibility.

3. **The New Beginning**: This is the stage where we emerge from the neutral zone with a renewed sense of purpose and direction. It's a time of exploration, experimentation, and the development of new skills and identities.

By understanding these stages and recognizing where we are in the transition process, we can approach change with greater self-compassion and clarity, allowing ourselves the time and space to process our emotions and prepare for what lies ahead.

Cultivating Resilience and Adaptability:

One of the key factors in navigating life's transitions successfully is the ability to be resilient and adaptable in the face of change.

Resilience is not about being invulnerable or immune to pain and difficulty, but rather about having the inner resources and coping strategies to bounce back from adversity and emerge stronger and more capable.

Some key practices for cultivating resilience include:

- **Developing a growth mindset**: Embracing challenges as opportunities for learning and growth, rather than threats to be avoided.

- **Practicing self-care**: Engaging in activities that nourish the body, mind, and spirit, such as exercise, meditation, and spending time in nature.

- **Building a support network**: Surrounding ourselves with people who can offer emotional support, practical assistance, and a fresh perspective.

- **Reframing setbacks**: Viewing failures and

disappointments as valuable learning experiences rather than personal shortcomings.

Adaptability, on the other hand, is about being flexible and responsive to the changing circumstances of our lives. It involves letting go of rigid expectations and being open to new possibilities and ways of being.

By cultivating adaptability, we can navigate transitions with greater ease and grace, embracing the uncertainty and unpredictability of life as an opportunity for growth and discovery.

Harnessing the Power of Meaning and Purpose:

One of the most powerful tools we have for navigating life's transitions is the ability to find meaning and purpose in the face of change and adversity. When we can connect our experiences of transition to a larger sense of meaning and purpose,

we can find the strength and resilience to persevere even in the face of great difficulty. This might involve reconnecting with our core values and beliefs, finding ways to contribute to something larger than ourselves, or engaging in practices that help us feel a sense of connection and belonging. It might also involve seeking out mentors, teachers, or role models who can inspire us and help us see the bigger picture. By harnessing the power of meaning and purpose, we can transform the challenges of transition into opportunities for growth, self-discovery, and the development of a deeper, more authentic sense of who we are and what we're here to do.

Embracing the Transformative Potential of Transition

Finally, it's important to recognize that life's transitions, while often difficult and painful, also hold the potential for profound transformation and growth. When we let go of the familiar and step into the unknown, we open ourselves up to new possibilities and ways of being. We have the opportunity to shed old patterns, beliefs, and identities that no longer serve us, and to cultivate new ways of thinking, feeling, and acting that are more aligned with our true nature and deepest values.

This process of transformation can be challenging and uncomfortable, but it's also a necessary part of the journey of personal growth and evolution. By embracing the transformative potential of transition, we can move through life's changes with a sense of curiosity, courage, and wonder, knowing that each transition is an opportunity to become more fully ourselves and to contribute to the world in a way that is uniquely ours.

Within conclusion

In conclusion, navigating life's transitions is a fundamental part of the human experience. While change can be difficult and disorienting, it also holds the potential for growth, self-discovery, and the development of a deeper, more authentic sense of who we are and what we're here to do.By cultivating the tools and strategies to navigate transitions with resilience and grace, we can not only survive but thrive in the face of change. We can learn to embrace uncertainty, to find meaning and purpose in the midst of adversity, and to transform the challenges of transition into opportunities for growth and renewal.

So let us approach life's transitions with courage, compassion, and a sense of adventure. Let us trust in our ability to adapt and grow, to find our way through the darkness and into the light. And let us remember that we are not alone in this journey – that we are part of a larger human family, all of us navigating the twists and turns of life together, supporting and uplifting one another along the way.

What role does emotional resilience play in navigating life's transitions: The emotional resilience plays a crucial role in successfully navigating life's transitions in several key ways:

1. Coping with Change and Uncertainty:

- Transitions often involve a significant amount of change and uncertainty, which can be psychologically and emotionally challenging.

- Emotionally resilient individuals are better able to adapt to these changes, manage their stress and anxiety, and maintain a sense of stability and purpose.

2. Bouncing Back from Setbacks:

- Life transitions can bring disappointments, losses, and setbacks. Emotionally resilient people are able to recover more quickly, learn from their experiences, and move forward with renewed determination.

- They are less likely to get stuck in negative thought patterns or become overwhelmed by difficult emotions.

3. Maintaining Perspective:

- Resilient individuals are able to maintain a broader perspective during times of transition, recognizing that challenges are temporary and that new opportunities often arise from change.

- This helps them avoid getting caught up in catastrophizing or rumination, and instead focus on constructive problem-solving.

4. **Seeking Support and Resources:**

- Emotionally resilient people are more likely to reach out for support from friends, family, or professionals during times of transition.

- They understand the importance of building a strong social support network and accessing the resources they need to navigate challenges successfully.

5. **Embracing Personal Growth:**

-Transitions often present opportunities for personal growth and transformation. Emotionally resilient individuals are able to view these changes as chances to learn, evolve, and become stronger versions of themselves.

-They are more open to new experiences and perspectives, and more willing to step outside their comfort zones. By cultivating emotional resilience through practices like stress management, self-care, and developing a growth mindset, individuals can better navigate the ups and downs of life's transitions. This allows all of us and them to emerge from these periods of change with a renewed sense of purpose, confidence, and the ability to adapt to whatever the future may hold.

Chapter 11

Purpose, and Fulfillment as a Universal Thread

The search for meaning, purpose, and fulfillment is a universal thread that binds us all together. As we navigate the ebbs and flows of our personal and professional journeys, the question of "Why am I here?" and "What is my true calling?" often arises, beckoning us to delve deeper into the rich, fertile soil of our own inner landscapes. In this chapter, we will embark on a transformative exploration of discovering your life's purpose – a journey that has the power to infuse your days with a renewed sense of passion, direction, and joy. Whether you are just starting out on your path or find yourself at a crossroads, the insights and strategies we will uncover together can serve as a guiding light, illuminating the way towards a life that is truly aligned with your deepest values and highest aspirations.

Uncovering Your Core Values

At the heart of discovering your life's purpose lies the cultivation of self-awareness – a deep, intimate understanding of who you are, what matters most to you, and the principles that guide your actions and decisions. By taking the time to reflect on your core values, you can begin to uncover the essential threads that weave together the tapestry of your life, providing a solid foundation upon which to build a purposeful and fulfilling existence.

Through exercises in self-reflection, journaling, and open-ended dialogue, you will have the opportunity to explore your innermost beliefs, desires, and motivations. What brings you a sense of joy and meaning? What causes or issues do you feel most passionately about? What legacy do you hope to leave behind? By delving into these questions with honesty and vulnerability, you can begin to distill the essence of who you are and what truly matters to you.

Aligning Your Passions and Talents: Once you have a clearer understanding of your core values, the next step in discovering your life's purpose is to explore the intersection of your passions and your unique talents and abilities. What activities or pursuits fill you with a sense of excitement, flow, and deep fulfillment? What skills and strengths do you possess that allow you to make a meaningful contribution to the world around you? By cultivating awareness of the things that ignite your inner fire and the areas in which you excel, you can begin to envision the ways in which you can leverage your gifts to create a life of purpose and impact.

This may involve exploring new career paths, volunteering or engaging in community service, or simply finding creative outlets that allow you to express your authentic self. Remember, the path to purpose is not always linear or straightforward. It may involve trial and error, unexpected twists and turns, and the willingness to step outside of your comfort zone. But by remaining open, curious, and committed to the process, you can uncover the unique calling that is yours to fulfill.

Embracing the Power of Contribution: As you delve deeper into the exploration of your life's purpose, you may find that the most fulfilling and meaningful pursuits are those that involve contributing to something larger than yourself. Whether it's working to address a pressing social or environmental issue, mentoring and supporting others, or using your talents to create art, music, or innovation that uplifts and inspires, the act of contribution can be a powerful antidote to feelings of disconnection, apathy, or lack of purpose. By shifting your focus outward and aligning your efforts with causes or communities that resonate with your values and passions, you can tap into a wellspring of energy, motivation, and a profound sense of belonging. This, in turn, can help you cultivate a deeper sense of meaning, purpose, and joy in your daily life – a virtuous cycle that can propel you forward on your path of personal and professional fulfillment.

Within Conclusion- Cultivating a Life of Purpose and Joy

In the end, the discovery of your life's purpose is not a destination to be reached, but a way of being – a lens through which you can view the world and your place in it. By cultivating self-awareness, aligning your passions and talents with meaningful contribution, and embracing the ebb and flow of your journey, you can create a life that is infused with a profound sense of meaning, purpose, and joy.

As you continue to nurture and tend to the rich, fertile landscape of your inner world, may you be inspired to share your unique gifts with the world, to uplift and empower those around you, and to leave an indelible mark on the tapestry of human experience. For in doing so, you not only fulfill your own deepest yearnings, but you also inspire others to do the same, creating a ripple effect of positive change that can transform lives and communities, one purposeful step at a time.

Key Steps to Discovering Your Life's Purpose

Reflect on Your Core Values: Take time to explore what matters most to you - what principles guide your actions and decisions? What causes or issues do you feel passionately about?

Identify Your Passions and Talents: What activities or pursuits fill you with a sense of joy and fulfillment? What skills and strengths allow you to make a meaningful contribution?

Explore the Intersection of Your Values, Passions and Talents: Look for ways to leverage your unique gifts in service of causes that resonate with your deepest beliefs. This intersection is often where your life's purpose lies.

Engage in Self-Reflection and Journaling: Use writing as a tool for uncovering your motivations, desires and the legacy you want to leave. Reflect on pivotal life experiences and how they've shaped you.

Seek Out New Experiences and Perspectives: Step outside your comfort zone and engage with people, ideas and activities that challenge your assumptions. This can spark new insights about your purpose.

Experiment and Iterate: Your sense of purpose may evolve over time. Be open to trying different paths and roles. Reflect on what feels most meaningful and makes the best use of your talents.

Consider How You Can Contribute to Something Larger Than Yourself: Aligning your efforts with causes that benefit others and the greater good can imbue your life with profound meaning and purpose.

Cultivate Patience and Self-Compassion - Discovering your purpose: Is a journey, not a destination. Trust the process, celebrate small steps forward, and treat yourself with kindness along the way.

Remember, your life's purpose is unique to you. By exploring your values, passions and talents with curiosity and an open heart, you can uncover the path that is yours to walk.

Deepening Your Connection to Purpose- Cultivating Mindfulness and Presence: As you embark on the journey of discovering your life's purpose, it is essential to develop the capacity for mindfulness and present-moment awareness. By training your mind to stay grounded in the here and now, you can gain deeper insights into your true desires, values, and sources of fulfillment. Through practices like meditation, breathwork, and mindful observation of your thoughts and sensations, you can learn to quiet the incessant chatter of the mind and tune into the subtle whispers of your inner wisdom. This heightened state of presence can help you recognize patterns, uncover hidden assumptions, and gain clarity on the direction that feels most aligned with your authentic self.

Moreover, mindfulness can cultivate a greater sense of self-compassion and patience as you navigate the ebbs and flows of the purpose-discovery process. Rather than berating yourself for not having all the answers, you can approach the journey with a spirit of curiosity, openness, and kindness towards yourself and your experience.

Cultivating Meaningful Connections

Another crucial aspect of discovering your life's purpose is the cultivation of meaningful connections with others. By engaging in deep, authentic dialogue with friends, family members, mentors, or like-minded individuals, you can gain valuable perspectives, insights, and support that can help you clarify and refine your sense of purpose.

These connections can take many forms – from formal mentorship relationships to casual conversations over coffee. The key is to seek out individuals who can offer a fresh, outside-the-box viewpoint, challenge your assumptions, and help you see your strengths, passions, and potential in a new light. Additionally, by engaging in community service, volunteering, or other forms of collaborative work, you can deepen your sense of connection to something larger than yourself. This can help you recognize the ways in which your unique gifts and talents can be leveraged to make a positive impact on the world around you.

Embracing the Power of Reflection in your daily life: One of the most powerful tools for discovering and deepening your connection to purpose is the practice of reflection and journaling. By setting aside dedicated time to explore your thoughts, feelings, and experiences through writing, you can uncover patterns, themes, and insights that may not be readily apparent in the hustle and bustle of daily life.

Whether you choose to write in a physical journal or use digital tools like online platforms or apps, the act of putting pen to paper (or fingers to keyboard) can help you process your emotions, clarify your values, and gain a clearer understanding of the direction you wish to take. Additionally, revisiting your journal entries over time can help you track your growth, identify areas of progress, and celebrate the small victories along the way.

Remember, the purpose-discovery process is not a linear one – it involves a constant cycle of reflection, experimentation, and adaptation. By embracing the power of journaling, you can create a space for self-exploration, self-expression, and the ongoing cultivation of your life's purpose.

Embracing the Journey of Purpose: Ultimately, the discovery and cultivation of your life's purpose is a lifelong journey – one that is marked by both triumphs and challenges, moments of clarity and periods of uncertainty. But by embracing the process with a spirit of curiosity, resilience, and self-compassion, you can unlock the profound joy, meaning, and fulfillment that comes from living a life that is truly aligned with your deepest values and highest aspirations.

Remember, your purpose is not a fixed destination, but a dynamic, ever-evolving expression of your authentic self. As you continue to explore, experiment, and grow, be open to the possibility that your purpose may shift and transform over time. Trust in the process, celebrate the small victories, and trust that each step you take is leading you closer to the life you were meant to live.

In the end, the journey of purpose is not just about finding your calling – it's about cultivating a deep, abiding connection to the essence of who you are, and using that connection to make a positive impact on the world around you. So embrace the adventure, trust the process, and let your purpose be the guiding light that illuminates your path.

The Impact of Self-Doubt on Purpose Discovery

Self-doubt can significantly impact the discovery of one's life's purpose in several key ways:

Inhibiting Exploration and Experimentation

Self-doubt can make people hesitant to try new things, step outside their comfort zones, or explore different paths that could lead to purpose.

Undermining Self-Awareness and Clarity

Persistent self-doubt can cloud one's ability to honestly reflect on their values, passions, and talents.

Fostering Indecision and Paralysis

Chronic self-doubt can lead to analysis paralysis, where individuals get stuck overthinking and second-guessing themselves rather than taking action.

Diminishing Motivation and Resilience

Self-doubt can sap one's motivation to pursue purpose-driven goals, as they may feel unworthy or incapable of achieving them.

Isolating the Individual

Persistent self-doubt can make people reluctant to seek support, guidance, or accountability from others. To overcome the detrimental effects of self-doubt, it's important for individuals to cultivate self-compassion, challenge negative patterns, and seek out mentors or support systems that can help bolster their confidence and self-belief. By doing so, they can create the conditions necessary to engage in the deep self-exploration and courageous action required to uncover their life's true purpose.

Long-Term Effects of Self-Doubt on Personal Growth: Some of the key long-term effects of self-doubt on personal growth include:

Stunted Confidence and Self-Believe: Chronic self-doubt can erode an individual's confidence in their abilities, making them less likely to take risks or pursue ambitious goals. This can lead to a self-fulfilling cycle where lack of confidence breeds more self-doubt.

Avoidance of Challenges and Opportunities: People plagued by self-doubt often shy away from new experiences, responsibilities, or chances for growth, fearing failure or inadequacy. This prevents them from developing new skills, expanding their horizons, and reaching their full potential.

The Impact of Self-Doubt on Purpose Discovery:

Self-doubt can significantly impact the discovery of one's life's purpose in several key ways:

Procrastination and Lack of Motivation:

Self-doubt can cause individuals to procrastinate on important tasks or projects, as they doubt their capacity to succeed.

This procrastination further reinforces the self-doubt, creating a vicious cycle of inaction and low motivation.

Stagnation and Missed Milestones:

The reluctance to take on new challenges or make changes can lead to professional and personal stagnation over time. Individuals may miss out on key milestones, promotions, or life experiences due to their self-doubt.

Negative Impact on Relationships:

Self-doubt can make it difficult for individuals to form and maintain healthy, supportive relationships, as they may struggle with vulnerability, trust, and communication. This can further exacerbate feelings of isolation and low self-worth.

Mental Health Issues: Prolonged self-doubt has been linked to the development of anxiety, depression, and other mental health concerns, which can further impede personal growth and well-being. To overcome these long-term effects, it's crucial for individuals to cultivate self-awareness, self-compassion, and strategies for challenging negative thought patterns. Seeking support from mentors, therapists, or supportive communities can also be instrumental in fostering the confidence and resilience needed for personal growth and fulfillment.

Chapter 12

Unlocking the Boundless Potential of the Mind

In the grand tapestry of human existence, the mind stands as our most powerful and versatile tool for navigating the complexities of life. With its unparalleled capacity for creativity, problem-solving, and self-discovery, the mind is the key that unlocks the doors to a world of infinite possibilities. Yet, despite its incredible potential, it is estimated that the average person utilizes only a fraction of their mental faculties on a daily basis. It's akin to having a brand-new Ferrari parked right outside your front door, but only having the skills to operate a bicycle.

As we embark on this journey of unlocking the boundless potential of the mind, it's crucial to understand that the mind is not a static entity, but rather a dynamic, ever-evolving landscape that responds to the ways in which we engage with it. By cultivating a deep understanding of the mind's architecture and the principles that govern its functioning, we can learn to harness its immense power and direct it towards the realization of our highest aspirations and most cherished dreams.

Anatomy of the Mind

To fully appreciate the potential of the mind, it's important to first understand its underlying structure and the various components that work together to create our subjective experience of reality. At the most fundamental level, the mind is composed of three interrelated parts: the conscious mind, the subconscious mind, and the unconscious mind.

The conscious mind is the part of our mental landscape that is actively engaged in the present moment, processing sensory information and engaging in rational thought. It is the part of the mind that we are most familiar with, as it is responsible for our day-to-day decision-making, problem-solving, and language processing.

The subconscious mind, on the other hand, operates beneath the surface of our conscious awareness, processing information and shaping our thoughts, emotions, and behaviors in ways that we may not always recognize.

It is the repository of our memories, habits, and learned patterns of behavior, and it plays a crucial role in shaping our overall sense of self and our place in the world.

Finally, the unconscious mind is the deepest and most mysterious layer of the mind, containing the primal drives, instincts, and archetypes that form the foundation of our psyche. While the unconscious mind is largely inaccessible to our conscious awareness, it nonetheless exerts a powerful influence on our thoughts, emotions, and behaviors, shaping our perceptions and experiences in ways that we may not fully understand.

The Power of Neuroplasticity

One of the most exciting and empowering discoveries in the field of neuroscience is the concept of neuroplasticity – the brain's remarkable ability to adapt, change, and rewire itself in response to new experiences and challenges.

This means that the mind is not a static entity, but rather a dynamic and malleable system that is constantly evolving and adapting to the demands of our environment and the choices we make. By harnessing the power of neuroplasticity, we can learn to reshape our neural pathways and create new patterns of thought, emotion, and behavior that are more aligned with our goals and values. This can involve engaging in practices like meditation, mindfulness, and cognitive-behavioral therapy, which have been shown to promote the growth of new neural connections and the strengthening of existing ones.

Moreover, neuroplasticity suggests that we are not limited by our genetic inheritance or our past experiences. Rather, we have the power to shape and mold our minds in ways that allow us to transcend our perceived limitations and unlock our full potential as human beings. By embracing the principles of neuroplasticity and committing to a regular practice of mental training and self-improvement, we can cultivate the mindset and skills needed to thrive in an ever-changing world.

The Importance of Mental Training: Just as physical fitness requires regular exercise and training, mental fitness is also a skill that must be developed and honed over time.

By engaging in a regular practice of mental training and self-reflection, we can learn to navigate the complexities of the mind with greater clarity, focus, and resilience. One of the most powerful tools for mental training is the practice of meditation. By learning to quiet the chatter of the mind and focus our attention on the present moment, we can cultivate a greater sense of self-awareness, emotional regulation, and cognitive control. Over time, a regular meditation practice can help us to break free from the grip of negative thought patterns, manage stress and anxiety more effectively, and tap into the wellspring of creativity and inspiration that lies at the heart of the mind.

In addition to meditation, there are many other forms of mental training that can help us to unlock the potential of the mind. These include practices like journaling, visualization, and goal-setting, which can help us to clarify our intentions, track our progress, and stay motivated on the path of personal growth and self-improvement.

As we continue to explore and expand the boundaries of the mind, it's important to recognize that the benefits of mental training extend far beyond the individual. By cultivating a greater sense of self-awareness, emotional intelligence, and cognitive flexibility, we can not only improve our own lives, but also contribute to the creation of a more just, equitable, and sustainable world.

Within Conclusion: Embracing the Adventure of the Mind

In the end, the journey of unlocking the boundless potential of the mind is not a destination to be reached, but an ongoing adventure to be savored and embraced. It is a path of self-discovery, growth, and transformation that requires courage, commitment, and a willingness to step outside our comfort zones and explore the uncharted territories of the psyche. As we continue to push the boundaries of what is possible, let us remember that the mind is not a fixed entity, but a dynamic, ever-evolving landscape that responds to the ways in which we engage with it. By cultivating a regular practice of mental training and self-reflection, we can learn to navigate the complexities of the mind with greater clarity, focus, and resilience, and unlock the full potential of our unique gifts and talents. So let us embrace the adventure of the mind with open hearts and curious minds, knowing that the journey itself is the true reward. Let us trust in the power of neuroplasticity and the transformative potential of mindful living, and let our efforts ripple outward, touching the lives of those around us and contributing to the creation of a better world for all.

Unlocking the Full Potential of the Mind: key ways to unlock the full potential of our minds

Embrace Neuroplasticity: Understand that the brain has an incredible capacity to adapt, change, and rewire itself throughout our lives (neuroplasticity). This means we are not limited by our genetic inheritance or past experiences, but have the power to shape and mold our minds in ways that allow us to transcend our perceived limitations.

Unlocking Your Mind's Potential

Are you ready to embark on a transformative journey of personal growth and self-discovery? Prepare to unlock the boundless potential of your mind and embrace the power of mental training and skill development. Let's dive in!

Engage in Mental Training and Skill Development:

- Treat your mind like a muscle that needs regular exercise and training to grow stronger.
- Engage in activities that challenge your cognitive abilities, such as learning a new language or skill.
- Consistently practice mental exercises to sharpen your focus, memory, and problem-solving skills.

Harness the Power of the Subconscious Mind:

- Recognize the immense influence of the subconscious mind on our thoughts, emotions, and behaviors.
- Explore techniques like meditation, visualization, and affirmations to tap into the power of your subconscious.
- Allow your subconscious to work in the background, providing insights and solutions to challenges.

Foster a Growth Mindset:

- Adopt the belief that intelligence and abilities are not fixed, but can be developed through effort and dedication.
- Embrace challenges as opportunities for growth and learning, rather than threats to your self-worth.
- Celebrate your progress and milestones, no matter how small, to build momentum and confidence.

Seek Out New Experiences and Perspectives:

- Expose yourself to diverse ideas, cultures, and ways of thinking to expand your mental horizons.
- Step outside your comfort zone and engage in activities that push you to think and act differently.

- Cultivate a beginner's mindset, always open to learning and growth.

Prioritize Self-Care and Wellbeing:

- Ensure you are getting enough sleep, nutrition, and physical activity to support optimal brain function.
- Practice stress management techniques to maintain a calm and focused mind.
- Surround yourself with a supportive network of friends, family, and mentors who encourage your growth.

By consistently applying these principles, you can unlock the boundless potential of your mind and embark on a transformative journey of personal growth, creativity, and self-actualization. The key is to approach this process with curiosity, commitment, and a willingness to step outside your comfort zone.

Distinguishing Healthy Resistance from Real Danger

As you navigate your path of personal growth, you may encounter moments of resistance or self-doubt. It's important to differentiate between healthy resistance that indicates growth and real danger that warrants caution. Let's explore some key ways to make this distinction:

Assess the Potential Consequences:

- If you move forward, what is the worst possible outcome? If it's not life-threatening or extremely detrimental, it's likely healthy resistance rather than real danger.

Examine the Source of the Fear:

- Is the fear coming from your ego trying to keep you in your comfort zone, or is it a genuine intuitive warning sign?
- Healthy resistance often stems from the ego's desire for safety and security.

Consider Your Past Experiences:

- Have you faced similar challenges before and come out okay on the other side?
- If so, it's a good sign the resistance is healthy growth pushing you to expand your limits.

Notice Your Body's Signals:

- Is your body reacting with the fight-or-flight response (racing heart, sweating, etc.)?

- This indicates real fear and potential danger. Healthy resistance may cause some discomfort but not an extreme stress response.

Reflect on Your Values:

- Is moving forward aligned with your core values and what you want for your life?
- If so, it's likely healthy resistance pushing you to grow and become your best self.

Consult Trusted Friends or Mentors:

- Talking it through with others can provide an outside perspective on whether your resistance is justified or just your ego talking.Trusted advisors can help you gain clarity and make empowered decisions.

The key is to approach the resistance with curiosity and self-compassion. Healthy resistance is a sign you are pushing your limits and expanding your comfort zone. Real danger warrants caution, but most of the time, the only thing holding us back is our own fear of failure or discomfort. Lean into the resistance and move forward anyway. This is where the magic of personal growth happens.

Chapter 13

The Imposter Syndrome

A Comprehensive Exploration of the Imposter Phenomenon and Its Impact on Healthcare Professionals. As a dedicated healthcare assistant, I sometimes assist very complex customer cases and have experienced moments of self-doubt and the nagging feeling that I am not truly qualified for the responsibilities I have taken on. This phenomenon, known as the "Imposter Syndrome," is a common experience among high-achieving individuals, including those in the healthcare field. In this chapter, we will delve into the intricacies of the Imposter Syndrome, its causes, and strategies to overcome this psychological hurdle.

Understanding the Imposter Syndrome

The Imposter Syndrome is a psychological pattern in which individuals, despite their evident accomplishments and qualifications, are unable to internalize their own success. They often attribute their achievements to luck, timing, or the efforts of others, rather than recognizing their own abilities and hard work. This can lead to a persistent fear of being exposed as a "fraud" and a constant struggle to prove one's worth. Causes and Manifestations of the Imposter Syndrome

The Imposter Syndrome can have various underlying causes, including:

1. **Perfectionism and High Expectation:** Healthcare professionals, driven by a desire for excellence, may set unrealistically high standards for themselves, leading to a constant feeling of falling short.

2. **Lack of Confidence and Self-Doubt:** Doubting one's own abilities and competence can be exacerbated by the demanding nature of the healthcare field, where the stakes are often high.

3. **Societal and Cultural Influences:** Societal and cultural expectations, particularly those related to gender and professional roles, can contribute to the development of the Imposter Syndrome.

The Imposter Syndrome can manifest in various ways, such as:

- Reluctance to take credit for one's achievements
- Constant fear of being exposed as a fraud
- Difficulty accepting praise or compliments
- Tendency to downplay one's successes
- Avoidance of challenging tasks or opportunities for growth

Overcoming the Imposter Syndrome: Fortunately, there are strategies you can employ to overcome the Imposter Syndrome and embrace your true capabilities.

1. **Acknowledge and Validate Your Accomplishments:** Take the time to reflect on your achievements and recognize the hard work and dedication that have led you to where you are today.

2. **Challenge Negative Self-Talk:** Be mindful of the internal dialogue that fuels the Imposter Syndrome and actively replace it with more positive and affirming self-talk.

3. **Seek Supportive Relationships:** Surround yourself with colleagues, mentors, and loved ones who can provide encouragement, validation, and a fresh perspective on your abilities.

4. **Embrace Mistakes and Failures as Learning Opportunities:** Reframe your perception of mistakes and failures, viewing them as chances to grow and improve, rather than as evidence of your inadequacy.

5. **Engage in Continuous Professional Development:** Ongoing learning and skill-building can help you build confidence and a stronger sense of competence in your field.

By understanding the Imposter Syndrome and implementing these strategies, you can overcome the self-doubt and embrace the true extent of your capabilities as a healthcare professional. Remember, you have earned your place and deserve to feel confident in your abilities to provide exceptional care to your patients.

The Impact of the Imposter Syndrome on Healthcare Professionals: The Imposter Syndrome can have significant effects on healthcare professionals, affecting their well-being, job satisfaction, and overall performance. Here are some of the ways in which the Imposter Syndrome can manifest in the healthcare setting:

1. **Reduced Job Satisfaction:** Healthcare professionals who experience the Imposter Syndrome may feel less fulfilled in their roles, leading to decreased job satisfaction and a higher likelihood of burnout.

2. **Increased Stress and Anxiety:** The constant fear of being exposed as a fraud can lead to chronic stress and anxiety, which can negatively impact both personal and professional life.

3. **Decreased Confidence in Decision-Making**

The Imposter Syndrome can undermine a healthcare professional's confidence in their decision-making abilities, potentially leading to hesitation or indecision in critical situations.

4. **Negative Impact on Patient Care:** When healthcare professionals are plagued by self-doubt and the Imposter Syndrome, it can negatively affect the quality of life of the

sufferer and the care they provide to patients. This can include delayed diagnoses, inadequate treatment plans, and reduced patient satisfaction.

Strategies for Managing the Imposter Syndrome in Healthcare: Given the significant impact of the Imposter Syndrome on healthcare professionals, it is essential to develop strategies for managing and overcoming this phenomenon.

Here are some practical tips

1. **Practice Self-Compassion:** Treat yourself with kindness and understanding, just as you would a patient. Recognize that everyone experiences self-doubt and that it is a normal part of the learning process.

2. **Focus on Your Strengths:** Identify and celebrate your strengths and accomplishments. This can help shift your focus away from perceived weaknesses and towards your true capabilities.

3. **Seek Feedback and Support:** Ask for feedback from colleagues and mentors, and seek support from those who can offer encouragement and validation.

4. **Engage in Mindfulness and Self-Care:** Regular mindfulness practices and self-care activities can help reduce stress and anxiety, allowing you to approach your work with a clearer mind.

5. **Celebrate Small Wins:** Acknowledge and celebrate small victories, no matter how minor they may seem. This can help build confidence and a sense of accomplishment.

Within conclusion: The Imposter Syndrome is a common phenomenon for most people living in our current daily society. It can affect anyone, even the most accomplished persons, as well the healthcare professionals. By understanding its causes and manifestations, and by implementing strategies to overcome it, you can reduce its impact and increase your job satisfaction, confidence, and overall well-being. Remember, you are capable and deserving of the respect and recognition you receive. Embrace your true capabilities and continue to provide exceptional care to your patients, by believing and trusting in yourself.

How can Care organizations support employees dealing with the imposter syndrome: Care organizations can support employees dealing with the imposter syndrome by implementing various strategies aimed at fostering an inclusive and supportive workplace culture. Here are some key approaches:

1. **Fostering an Inclusive Workplace:**

- Celebrate Diversity and Inclusion: Ensure that all employees feel valued and included, regardless of their background or role. This can be achieved by promoting diversity, equity, and inclusion (DEI) initiatives and creating a culture where everyone feels welcome and respected.

2. **Creating a Supportive Workplace Culture:**

- Open Communication and Feedback: Encourage open communication and feedback to create a safe space for employees to discuss their challenges, including the imposter syndrome.
- This can help employees feel more comfortable in sharing their concerns and seeking support.

3. Providing Training for Managers:

- Manager Training: Educate managers on the signs of imposter syndrome and coach them to engage with employees who experience self-doubt. This can help employees manage their feelings of inadequacy and differentiate between real and perceived shortcomings.

4. Building Relationships and Trust:

- **Mentoring and Social Activities**: Develop relationships between employees from the beginning, such as through mentoring programs or social activities. This can help employees feel more comfortable discussing their struggles and seeking support from colleagues.

5. Emphasizing Growth and Learning Over Perfection:

- **Growth and Learning**: Shift the focus from perfection to growth and learning.

  This can help employees feel more comfortable taking risks and trying new things without feeling like they have to prove themselves constantly.

6. Recognizing and Validating Employees' Accomplishments:

- **Public Acknowledgment:** Regularly acknowledge employees' hard work and accomplishments publicly. This can help individuals attribute their successes to their own efforts and build confidence.

7. Ensuring Fair Compensation and Job Fit:

- **Fair Compensation**: Ensure that compensation packages are fair and commensurate with the market rate for specific jobs. This can help alleviate feelings of being over rewarded or underqualified, which can contribute to imposter syndrome.

8. Reframing Beliefs and Limiting Thoughts:

- Education and Awareness: Educate employees about imposter syndrome and the common thought patterns associated with it. This can help individuals reframe their beliefs and recognize that they are not alone in experiencing these feelings.

9. Encouraging Internal Motivation:

- Intrinsic Motivation: Help employees connect with their internal motivators and intrinsic values. This can boost their confidence and sense of purpose, reducing feelings of inadequacy.

10. Addressing Workplace Biases and Gaslighting:

- Transparency and Accountability: Address workplace biases and gaslighting by being transparent about hurdles and biases. This can help build trust and ensure that employees feel supported and valued, regardless of their background.

By implementing these strategies, organizations can create a supportive environment that helps employees overcome imposter syndrome and thrive in their roles.

Chapter 14

The Universe Wants You to be in Abundance, with Purpose, and Dignified

Embracing a Mindset of Abundance, Purpose, and Dignity. As a dedicated healthcare professional, I have encountered moments of self-doubt, scarcity, and a sense of unworthiness. However, it is crucial to understand that the universe, in its infinite wisdom, desires for you to live a life of abundance, purpose, and dignity. In this chapter, we will explore the transformative power of this mindset and how it can positively impact your personal and professional journey.

The Abundance Mindset: Cultivating a Prosperity Mindset

The abundance mindset is a fundamental shift in perspective that allows you to recognize and embrace the infinite possibilities available to you.

This mindset is rooted in the belief that there is more than enough for everyone, and that you are deserving of success, fulfillment, and prosperity. By cultivating an abundance mindset, you can:

1. **Overcome Limiting Beliefs:** Identify and challenge the limiting beliefs that may have been holding you back, such as the fear of failure or the belief that resources are scarce.

2. **Shift Your Focus:** Direct your attention towards opportunities, rather than obstacles, and see challenges as chances for growth and learning.

3. **Embrace Gratitude:** Cultivate a deep sense of gratitude for the blessings and abundance already present in your life, which can open the door to even greater abundance.

Finding Your Purpose: Aligning Your Work with Your Passions: Discovering and aligning your work with your deeper purpose is a powerful way to find meaning, fulfillment, and a sense of dignity in your healthcare career. By connecting with your purpose, you can:

1. **Tap into Your Intrinsic Motivation:** Identify the core values and passions that drive you, and use them to guide your professional decisions and actions.

2. **Contribute to Something Greater:** Recognize that your work as a healthcare professional is not just a job, but a calling to make a positive impact on the lives of others.

3. **Develop a Sense of Meaning and Fulfillment:** When your work is aligned with your purpose, you are more likely to experience a deep sense of meaning and fulfillment, which can enhance your overall well-being and job satisfaction.

Embracing Dignity- Honoring Yourself and Your Profession: Dignity is the inherent worth and respect that every individual deserves, regardless of their circumstances or achievements. As a healthcare professional, it is essential to cultivate a sense of dignity, both for yourself and for the profession you have chosen. By embracing dignity, you can:

1. **Stand Tall and Proud:** Recognize your own worth and value, and carry yourself with confidence and self-assurance.

2. **Advocate for Your Profession:** Actively promote the importance and dignity of the healthcare profession, and work to address any stigma or misconceptions.

3. **Treat Others with Respect and Compassion:** Extend the same level of dignity and respect that you desire for yourself to your patients, colleagues, and the broader community.

Integrating the Sense of Abundance, Purpose, and Dignity into Your Life: To fully embrace the mindset of abundance, purpose, and dignity, it is essential to integrate these principles into your daily life and professional practice. Here are some strategies to help you achieve this:

1. **Engage in Regular Self-Reflection:** Set aside time for introspection, to examine your beliefs, values, and the alignment between your work and your purpose.

2. **Surround Yourself with Supportive Influences:** Seek out mentors, colleagues, and resources that reinforce the abundance mindset and your sense of purpose and dignity.

3. **Continuously Develop and Grow:** Engage in ongoing learning, skill-building, and professional development to enhance your capabilities and deepen your sense of purpose.

4. **Practice Self-Care and Mindfulness:** Incorporate self-care practices, such as meditation, exercise, and leisure activities, to maintain my physical, mental, and emotional well-being.By embracing the mindset of abundance, purpose, and dignity, I finally unlock my full potential, have find greater fulfillment in my healthcare career, and inspire those around me to do the same. Remember, the universe wants you to thrive, and by aligning your thoughts and actions with this truth, you can create a life of abundance, purpose, and dignity, as I reckon have achieved along my paths at the end of the day.

Draw From Your Own Experiences

- Reflect on your own journey as a healthcare professional and the emotions you've experienced - the challenges, triumphs, moments of doubt and inspiration. Tap into those authentic feelings to infuse yourself with strong emotion and courage.

Abundance- Cultivating a Mindset of Prosperity

- The abundance mindset is a transformative perspective that allows you to recognize the boundless opportunities available to you. It is a shift away from scarcity thinking and towards a belief in the infinite potential that surrounds you.

By embracing this mindset, you can

- Overcome limiting beliefs that can hold you back, and replace them with empowering thoughts of possibility and growth.
- Focus your attention on the abundance of resources, support, and potential that exists, rather than dwelling on perceived obstacles.
- Cultivate a deep sense of gratitude for the blessings already present in your life, which can open the door to even greater abundance.

Purpose- Aligning Your Work with Your Passions

- Your work as a healthcare professional is not just a job, but a calling to make a positive impact on the lives of others.

By connecting with your deeper purpose, you can

- Tap into your intrinsic motivation, drawing inspiration from the core values and passions that drive you.

- Recognize that your contributions, no matter how small, are part of a greater mission to improve the well-being of your community and the world.

- Experience a profound sense of meaning and fulfillment, which can enhance your overall job satisfaction and personal well-being.

Dignity: Honoring Yourself and Your Profession

- Dignity is the inherent worth and respect that every individual deserves, and as a healthcare professional, it is essential that you cultivate a deep sense of dignity for both yourself and your chosen profession. By embracing dignity, you can:

- Stand tall and proud, recognizing your own value and worth, and carrying yourself with confidence and self-assurance.

- Actively promote the importance and dignity of the healthcare profession, addressing any stigma or misconceptions that may exist.

- Extend the same level of respect and compassion that you desire for yourself to your patients, colleagues, and the broader community.

Integrating Abundance, Purpose, and Dignity into Your Life

- To fully harness the transformative power of the abundance, purpose, and dignity mindset, it is crucial to integrate these principles into your daily life and professional practice. By engaging in regular self-reflection, surrounding yourself with supportive influences, continuously developing and growing, and practicing self-care and mindfulness, you can:
- Deepen your understanding of your own values, beliefs, and the alignment between your work and your purpose.
- Cultivate a network of mentors, colleagues, and resources that reinforce your abundance mindset and sense of dignity.
- Enhance your capabilities and expertise, further solidifying your sense of purpose and contribution.
- Maintain your physical, mental, and emotional well-being, ensuring that you have the resilience and energy to thrive in your healthcare career.

- Remember, the universe has bestowed upon you the gifts of abundance, purpose, and dignity. By embracing these qualities and integrating them into your life, you can unlock your full potential, find greater fulfillment in your daily life, your goals, and in the healthcare career as well, and inspire those around you to do the same. Embark on this transformative journey with a heart filled with gratitude, purpose, and a deep sense of your own worth and dignity.

The Epilogue: A Heartfelt Conclusion

As I reflect on the journey we've shared through the pages of this book, I am filled with a profound sense of gratitude. My name is Lea Monera, and at the age of 61, I humbly stand before you as a resident of a small hamlet in the province of Alicante, Spain. Throughout this work, I have poured my heart and soul, driven by a deep-rooted desire to share the wisdom and insights I have gathered over the years. At the core of this book lies a fundamental truth: that we are all connected, not just as individuals, but as part of a larger tapestry of humanity. As a caring, generous, and responsible person, I have always believed in the power of respect – respect for others and, most importantly, respect for ourselves. It is this guiding principle that has shaped the narrative you have experienced. Through the 14 chapters, I have endeavored to weave a tapestry of knowledge, personal anecdotes, and heartfelt reflections. My hope is that each reader, regardless of their background or life experiences, will find something that resonates deeply within you. Whether it's a newfound appreciation for the beauty of our natural world, a deeper understanding of the human condition, or simply a renewed sense of purpose. My greatest wish is that this book will leave an indelible mark on your heart and mind. As we part ways, I invite you to carry the lessons learned within these pages with you, to cherish the moments of connection, and to embrace the power of kindness and respect in all that you do. For it is through these simple yet profound acts that we can truly transform the world around us, one heart at a time. Thank you, my dear readers, for embarking on this journey with me. May the words within these pages continue to inspire and guide you, long after the final page has been turned.

" With my kind regards, all of my love and gratitude"

Author: Lea Monera

Written on June 29, 2024

in The Vereda de los Cubos

Callosa de Segura (Alicante) Spain